Dedication

This book is dedicated to

Henry J. Marks

Without whose help the implementation of the truths of this book would have been delayed several years.

A
Banker's Confession:

A Christian Guide to Getting Out of Debt

by Gary Sanseri

Back Home Industries
P. O. Box 22495
Portland, OR 97222

A Banker's Confession
© 1991 by Gary Sanseri
Published by Back Home Industries
P.O. Box 22495; Portland, Oregon 97222

All rights reserved. No part of this book may be reproduced or transmitted in any form or by any means without permission in writing from the Publisher

Printed in the United States of America

ISBN 1-880045-06-0

Acknowledgments

I especially want to thank the following individuals for their contribution in the production of this book.

Gregg Harris for giving me the idea for such a project.

Dan Vaughan for his solid convictions to live debt free and for his helpful, editorial suggestions.

My wife, **Wanda**, who has greatly encouraged me to utilize my writing abilities. She has been a real helper.

The LORD Jesus Christ, without whom we can do nothing.

Table of Contents

Chapter 1	My Personal Struggle With Debt	11
Chapter 2	We Owe It To Ourselves	19
Chapter 3	The Enslaving Power Of Debt	29
Chapter 4	Other Hazards Of Debt	41
Chapter 5	The History Of Usury: Part One Ancient Times To Christ	57
Chapter 6	The History Of Usury: Part Two The Early Church To Modern Times	75
Chapter 7	The Marvel Of Loan Pre-Payment	93
Chapter 8	The Value Of Thrift	107
Chapter 9	Investing For The Future	123
End Notes		141
Appendix A	Scripture Index	169
	Sample Amortization Schedule	175
	Sample Loan Payment Schedule With $25.00 Prepayment	185
	Sample Loan Payment Schedule With $50.00 Prepayment	193
	Sample Loan Payment Schedule With $100.00 Prepayment	201
	Sample Loan Payment Schedule With $200.00 Prepayment	207

Introduction

After finishing two years of college, I decided I needed to find a full time job. My major field of interest and training happened to be business and accounting. At the time I had a relative who worked for a large, local bank so I went and visited him and inquired what the chances might be for my obtaining a job at the bank. He introduced me to a gentleman in the personnel department and within a week I was working my first full time job.

My first position entailed working nights as a batch clerk, processing checks generated by the various branches of the bank. My career progressed to Assistant Supervisor in the Central Cash Vault and Assistant Operations Officer at one of the branches in the downtown area. It was here that I experienced my first real understanding of the banking function and how the loan process fits into the operations of the bank.

Initially, my intention for working in the branch was to receive training in branch operations and then advance to the position of loan officer. I learned early that to make it to the top in banking one must know the loan making process and obtain a good working knowledge of handling loans.

Before long I observed the stress and added responsibility endured by branch operations officers and loan officers. Additionally, I was beginning to learn, as a new Christian, the dangers of borrowing money and paying interest. I concluded that encouraging people to go into debt was not the best vocation for me.

This book is written with the goal of helping and encouraging Christians to take the necessary steps to get out of debt and live entirely debt free. Our policy, at Back Home Industries, is to operate our business by the principles written in this book. These same principles are practiced in our home finances, so we know they work.

Gary Sanseri

Chapter One
My Personal Struggle With Debt

A dollar a day can save the average homeowner
$44,671
in interest payments to the bank!

No bank advertisement proclaims: "Make the bank rich at your own expense," or "Increase years of debt with little benefit to yourself."

For years, even as a banker, I did not realize how much money a person with a loan could save through small prepayments. For example, by simply adding $30 a month (or $1 a day) to the monthly mortgage payment, a family with a $100,000 loan at 10.5% interest for 30 years can reduce the term of their debt by five years and save $44,671 painlessly! Incredible! And the theory does not just apply to homeowners. Anyone with a loan, whether it be for a car, home repair, or college tuition can benefit from this secret.

The major portion of early loan payments are applied to interest. The bank computes monthly interest due on the outstanding balance. What most of us do not know is that by reducing the balance sooner with additional payments, we prevent the bank from recharging interest on that amount month after month and year after year. If we can regularly pay an additional amount on the principle (even a small amount) we can save thousands of dollars.

If it is so simple to make such dramatic savings,

why do only 5% of Americans pre-pay loans? We accept debt as normal, but is it? Have we been deceived? Have the facts been purposefully withheld?

Like most Americans, my wife and I overextended ourselves to buy a dream house. Granted the price of the home was more than we planned to pay, but we thought we could use the bigger yard and additional floor space with our large family. Besides a second mortgage at 9% interest sounded like a bargain. Our home would increase in value every year, or so we thought, and we knew our rental house would sell any day. We could pay the debt on our residence from the profit we would gain from this sale.

Nothing happened the way we planned. The second property remained unsold. In order to meet the monthly mortgage payments still owed to the bank, we were forced to rent it out.

Tenant after tenant defaulted on payments or moved without giving notice. Some months the house remained vacant while we interviewed new prospective renters. We spent hours cleaning up the messes left behind. One family, rather than pay their monthly sanitation expenses, saved six months of garbage in plastic bags. They left the accumulation of rotting food and moldy trash for us to discard.

Unanticipated major repairs sapped the small profit we expected. We had to rebuild the motor to the furnace and reroof the garage. An electrical short was discovered. Plumbing problems occurred. The frustrations seemed endless.

We did not collect enough rent to cover our expenses. We had presumed on the future counting on our equity from this house to help us pay off our new home. Instead we were losing money! To top things off both our houses were depreciating! According to the new assessment from the tax collector our dream home was now worth $80,800.00, a 15.8% decrease from its earlier assessment of $96,000.00.

In the midst of our discouragement, a Christian economist asked us a probing question, "How would you like the peace of mind knowing you owe nothing to anyone, not even a mortgage to the bank? How would you like to be totally debt free?"

The idea of complete financial freedom in America sounded like a fairy tale to us, but we could tell he was serious. He actually thought we could be unshackled from all debt. Could it be possible? It was a new thought, an exciting thought, a vision that pressed us to action.

Debt on real estate had been presented to us as part of the American way of life. "Did anyone in our country own their home before retirement?" we rationalized.

We had been taught that borrowing money for depreciating goods like appliances or clothes was foolish and we had avoided credit card debt. We drove used cars that we purchased with cash. But we had never questioned the wisdom of borrowing for items like property that supposedly appreciate in value.

For the first time we asked ourselves if we had bought into a lie. Does real estate always increase in value? Did the Bible exclude property mortgage in the warnings against debt? We knew of numerous foreclosures in our own city. Our own houses had steadily dropped in value. Trends throughout the country indicated similar situations happening elsewhere.

We began to recognize the weight of our indebtedness. I wanted to change jobs but starting a new venture would cut my income. The obligations on the house restricted me from changing my career and making less money. I felt enslaved to my creditors. When we bought the property we thought an extra $25,000 debt would be easy to handle. Now, after just two years, our outstanding balance was reduced by a mere $2,000. By the time we fulfilled our obligation, we would pay over $40,000 in principal and interest.

Our friend suggested that we begin to prepay the mortgage on our home and relieve the debt as soon as possible. We took his advice and began making an additional fifty to seventy-five dollar principal paymenteach month. As a result we saved thousands of dollars, cut seven years off our mortgage schedule, and best of all, I was free to make the job change I desired.

Real Estate Trends

America, like the rest of the world, faces a mounting financial crises. We have become the greatest debtor nation on the globe and under current national policy and practice the problem continues to escalate. As a nation America is over spent and under saved.

Economists generally agree that an economic

transition lies ahead. Some of the more optimistic ones believe the transition will be relatively easy with very little change in our current spending habits. A second group, not quite as confident, feels that a period of mild adjustments and possibly a minor recession is in store. The last group of economists are the pessimists who see nothing but trouble ahead. They're preparing for a violent recession or even another "Great Depression". Which group is correct? Nobody knows for sure, but they all agree we can no longer spend our way into prosperity.

Real estate has been greatly affected by this economic crises. Recently my wife and I visited our local banker who told us that some 800 home owners in Alaska could no longer handle their mortgage payments and they simply turned their keys over to the bank and left the state. This amazing figure represents just one of the major banks in Alaska.

According to Donald McAlvany "the United States real estate market is in the early stages of a colossal bust. It is vastly over-built, over-priced, over-mortgaged and vulnerable to a major collapse." Already in Arizona housing prices have dropped 25% and in Colorado they're down 30%. [1] Similar trends have occurred in Texas, and the Pacific Northwest.

Ron Blue recalls the real estate boom in Atlanta during the early 1970's when investors followed the "Great Fool Theory". "It doesn't make any difference what I pay for a piece of property, because there's a bigger fool than I am who will pay even more for it." "Unfortunately, that didn't continue to be true, and many Christian (as well as non-Christian) investors consequently lost fortunes."[2]

McAlvany continues his report by showing how "a new study from the National Bureau of Economic Research projects that... home prices in the United States should decline steadily for the next 18 years, dropping off 47% in real terms ." He concludes that "the family home over the next 15 years is going to be one of the worst investments to own."[3] Mr. McAlvany, on a radio broadcast, offered to sell his home in Colorado because he would rather rent. Another author, likewise a resident of Colorado, wrote "I watched the value of my condominium in Denver deflate from $132,000.00 in 1982 to about $85,000.00 in 1988, and it is still going down." [4]

Unfortunately some financial advisors do not see the dangerous trends in real estate investments. They encourage credit worthy customers to use leverage to purchase homes and rental property. Howard Ruff defines leverage as "the principle of multiplying one's strength beyond one's natural capabilities... The lever that multiplies your financial strength is usually borrowed money."[5]

Another advisor recommends taking advantage of leverage "so that you may use other people's money to make money for yourself, just like the banks do." [6] The use of leverage necessitates the extension of credit. Once credit is extended a debt incurs which the borrower must repay.

The intention of leverage simply stated is to "purchase something with someone else's money, let it appreciate, then sell it at a profit." [7] This concept sounds good and sometimes can result in financial success. However it is based upon several faulty presumptions.

First, **using leverage assumes that all real estate always appreciates.** We have already shown the fallacy of this notion. Numerous families and individuals like us have discovered the hard way that property does not always increase in value.

Second, **borrowing money to purchase real estate assumes there will always be a market for the sale of your investment.** One real estate developer made over $1 million per year. He recounted, "Anybody could have made money during times of inflation if they were willing to take the risk of high leverage." [8] "Unfortunately for him, the economy in his area turned bad when he was most highly leveraged, and he was unable to sell the properties he had accumulated." [9]

Third, **because leverage is debt, it presumes on the future.** In the case above the real estate broker assumed the market would remain the same and inflation would continue. Furthermore, he did not count the cost of his obligations in case of unplanned catastrophes. As a result "he was also unable to continue making the debt payments on those properties" and was forced to file bankruptcy.[10]

Finally, **borrowing money instead of paying cash assumes you will be able to earn a higher interest rate than the rate on your loan.** Most home mortgage rates run higher than the interest rates paid on safe investments. To earn a greater return on your money you would have to invest it at comparatively high risk. Howard Ruff says "the risks of leverage vary greatly depending on the investment...but all forms of leverage are volatile and should be considered only if you have risk capital and the ability to sleep at night despite having invested your money at substantial risk." [11] If one has risk capital on hand why not instead pay cash and remain debt and worry free?

As Christians it is imperative that we take immediate steps to reduce our susceptibility to the myth of continued home appreciation. Things do not appreciate forever. Those in debt will be the first to suffer financial ruin in times of recession and depression. Wise stewards of earthly wealth will take personal responsibility for their future economic stability by getting out of debt now!

The purpose of this book is to arouse you to debt free living. I will share the secrets I learned that helped us pay off our loans early. To put these financial issues in biblical perspective, I will also discuss the historic view of the church on interest and debt. We will review ideas we have learned for stretching money and suggest ways to invest the surplus you will naturally aquire from following these principles. You may have never heard some of these things before, but I trust you will be challenged to take the necessary action, so you too can experience financial freedom.

Chapter Two
We Owe It To Ourselves

"Our national debt after all is an internal debt owed not only by the nation but to the nation. If our children have to pay interest on it they will pay that interest to themselves."

-*Franklin D. Roosevelt-*

The winter of 1783 brought a different kind of chill to the American Congress. The British troops were withdrawing from American soil after a long bloody battle. Instead of celebration in the victorious Continental Army, a conspiracy brewed in the town of Newburgh, New York. A military coup seemed inevitable!

A committee of officers headed by Major Alexander McDougall, Major John Armstrong and General Horatio Gates sent a petition to Congress demanding the payment of all back salaries to its soldiers. The rightful pay owed by Congress was seriously in arrears. As a result of the war for American independence, the Confederacy was deep in debt with no means to settle its accounts. If Congress refused to pay, the delegation would encourage their "fellow officers into issuing a defiant declaration." [1]

If successful the Continental Army would refuse to lay down its arms and continue to function as a military threat until paid in full. An anonymous circular stated, "the men who had saved the country were being deserted by the very rulers who had called on them to fight." 2

Armstrong called for a meeting of the officers to decide on the action they would take. Without the consent of the Commander-In-Chief, George Washington, such a meeting was illegal. Washington, recognizing the threat to his country, "issued an order forbidding the unauthorized meeting...and proposed instead a regular meeting of the officers for a discussion of grievances." 3

Washington's actions were interpreted by the dissenters as endorsing or "sanctifying" their scheme. On Saturday, March 15th, the officers met as planned. However, the unexpected appearance of General Washington caused the group to murmur and stir. As he waited for the audience to quiet, Washington looked at the frowning faces of those whom he led for six years in a war which seemed hopeless to win. Now he feared doing battle with them.

As the general began to read his speech the paper in his hand shook. "This dreadful alternative, of either deserting our Country (by moving to the unsettled Western lands) in the extremest hour of her distress, or turning our arms against it (which is the apparent object, unless Congress can be compelled into instant compliance) has something so shocking in it, that humanity revolts at the idea." 4 "He begged the officers to be patient, to trust their government. In time, he assured them, Congress would find ways of paying them." 5

Washington then drew out of his pocket a second piece of paper containing a letter from Congress explaining their attempts to settle the officers' grievances. After reading the first paragraph he paused and took from another pocket his spectacles which few of the men had ever seen. According to Major Samuel Shaw who observed the event, Washington, "begged the indulgence of his audience while he put them on, observing at the same time that he had grown gray in their service, and now found himself growing blind." [6]

Historian, Clarence Carson notes that "the eyes of those gathered round filled with tears, for they knew how sturdily he had borne so much for so many years." [7] The officers immediately abandoned their scheme and affirmed their confidence in Congress. "Washington's timely intervention prevented what could have been a military coup." [8]

Debt in America

This story from the life of George Washington illustrates what can happen when debt accumulates. By the end of the war for American independence the total debt of the Confederacy climbed to over $35 million. [9] To add to the problem Congress attempted to finance the debt with large issues of paper money. As in all paper money schemes, inflation (an increase in the money supply) emerged and resulted in price increases. This in turn stifled production and the economy, climaxing in a full-fledged depression in 1784. In the state of Massachusetts mobs (known as

Shay's Rebellion) prevented courts from convening to keep judges from foreclosing on heavily indebted farm land. [10]

Between 1775 and 1779, Congress authorized the printing of $241,552,780.00 in paper currency. [11] Attempts to support the scheme failed and the value of the paperbacks depreciated rapidly. The chart below details the declining worth of the Continental dollar. [12]

<u>Depreciation of the Continental 1779</u>

January 14	8 to 1
February 3	10 to 1
April 2	17 to 1
May 5	24 to 1
June 4	20 to 1
September 17	24 to 1
October 14	30 to 1
November 17	38 to 1

By January of 1781 the value dropped to 100 to 1. Pelatiah Webster declared, "it ceased to pass as currency, but was afterwards bought and sold as an article of speculation, at very uncertain and desultory (random) prices, from five hundred to one thousand to one." [13] These vain attempts by government to help the economy escalated the problem and prolonged the elimination of the war debt.

Currently the United States Government operates on a deficit (spending more than you have) basis. In 1987 Hans Sennholz noted that government over spent its budget 24 of the last 25 years.[14] The following chart helps illustrate the magnitude of the growing debt problem in America.

Growth of Federal Debt
(In **millions** of U.S. dollars)

Year	Dollar	Year	Dollar
1791	75	1900	1,263
1802	81	1905	1,132
1815	100	1910	1,147
1820	91	1915	1,191
1825	84	1920	24,299
1830	49	1925	20,516
1835	0	1930	16,185
1840	4	1935	28,701
1845	16	1940	42,968
1850	63	1945	258,682
1855	36	1950	257,377
1860	65	1955	274,418
1865	2,678	1960	284,700
1870	2,436	1965	313,819
1875	2,156	1970	370,094
1880	2,091	1975	533,189
1885	1,579	1980	914,300
1890	1,122	1985	1827,500
1895	1,097	1987	2255,893

Source: Hans Sennholz, *Debts and Deficits*, p. 73.

In real 1987 monetary terms it would take $2,400 additional tax on each American household to cover government overspending its budget. Furthermore, to pay off the Federal debt would cost each man, woman and child in the United States ten thousand dollars. 15

But before we cast stones, let's look at the amount of consumer debt in America. Statistics from the Board of Governors of the Federal Reserve System state that individual consumer debt, including home mortgage debt, amounts to $2 trillion and debts to businesses and corporations add up to another $2.4 trillion. Debts of state and local governments come to another $559 billion. 16

When the Honorable Stephen Allen of New York died there was found in his pocket a list of printed rules which guided his life. Among these precepts he listed "earn your money before you spend it" and "live within your income." 17 These words may seem redundant to Americans yet few of us heed them as did Stephen Allen.

But We Owe It to Ourselves

For the last 60 years, since the days of Franklin Roosevelt's New Deal, Americans have followed the economic idea of "buy now, pay later." This philosophy, taught by many economists, has lead our country into a spendthrift mentality which says we can spend our way to prosperity and it's all right to spend more money than we possess. After all, they rationalize, "we owe it to ourselves."

Those who promote this teaching believe that the money borrowed internally from citizens to finance government does not incur any real costs. If this is true then we can conclude that government debt does not matter. Any interest paid by the government on loans made internally simply transfers funds from taxpayers to bondholders.

But as Hans Sennholz notes, "we do not owe these sums to ourselves, the U.S. government owes them to individual savers and investors. The 'now generation' that consumes the savings creates debt obligations and expects future generations to pay them....A government debt is a government claim against personal income and private property - an unpaid tax bill so to speak - that will fall due in the future." [18]

This principle holds true for private debt. Any purchase made with money you do not have must be paid with future earnings. Those who choose deficit spending pre-commit their income and they mortgage their future. You do not owe this money to yourself, you owe it to your creditor.

Everyone Wants a Piece of the Pie

Much of government debts and deficits today are a direct result of the "welfare state." I have personally talked with many who voice disgust and concern over government extravagance and spending programs to help the "needy." Indeed, many believe our current economic system cannot last forever and that collapse is imminent. Americans generally agree that federal spending must drastically be reduced. However, when thinking of cutting specific federally financed programs people begin to hesitate. They fear their piece of the pie will be taken away. Everyone hopes that someday they too can get in on government handouts.

According to Dr. Sennholz a nationwide poll revealed that Americans are alarmed about the national debt and federal deficits but "resist any attempt at reducing federal spending." [19] The statistics are shocking! "Spending cuts could adversely affect some 90 million Americans who depend on government dollars for support." [20]

Thirty five million elderly receive old-age social security, railroad, veterans, federal civil service, and state and local retirement benefits. Nine million receive survivor benefits. Six million benefit from supplemental income programs. Six million unemployed individuals receive unemployment benefits while some two million men and women draw armed services pay. More than sixteen million government employees support some twenty million dependents. [21] The end product of these federally financed programs is massive federal deficits and a growing national debt.

Conclusion

On June 14, 1783 General George Washington issued a circular to be read in all the states. In this document he declared four essential things for the well being and existence of the United States as an Independent power. The second of these states "a sacred regard to Public Justice." 22

To Washington, this included rendering complete justice to all the Public Creditors. He described what he meant by saying, "the ability of the Country to discharge the debts which have been incurred in its defence, is not to be doubted...the path of our duty is plain before us; honesty will be found on every experiment, to be the best and only true policy; let us then as a Nation be just; let us fulfil the public Contracts, which Congress had undoubtedly a right to make for the purpose of carrying on the War, with the same good faith we suppose ourselves bound to perform our private engagements." 23

Unfortunately we have not followed Washington's advice. As Dr. Sennholz notes, "even the pledge of repayment can no longer be taken seriously, as new debt is added every day, and the mountain of debt surpasses all possibilities of repayment." 24 Such irresponsibility would never be tolerated in the private sector. Any politician who handled his own financial affairs the way government handles theirs would soon find himself bankrupt.

Debt, both public and private, has become a national threat to American production, growth, security, peace and strength. America is vulnerable to withdrawal by foreign investors, complete credit collapse, recession, reformation of the debt structure, protectionism, and more government taxation, inflation and regulation. 25

In his farewell address in 1796, President Washington declared, "as a very important source of strength and security, cherish public credit. One method of preserving it is to use it as sparingly as possible; avoiding occasions of expence by cultivating peace, but remembering also that timely disbursements to prepare for danger frequently prevent much greater disbursements to repel it; avoiding likewise the accumulation of debt, not only by shunning occasions of expence, but by vigorous exertions in time of Peace to discharge the Debts which unavoidable wars may have occasioned, not ungenerously throwing upon posterity the burthen which we ourselves ought to bear." [26]

    The following chapters will attempt to encourage us to heed some of Washington's advice. Credit should be used very sparingly as the extension of credit leads to debt. The accumulation of debt must be avoided. As responsible Christians we cannot mortgage our future and strap our children with the financial burdens we should bear.

Chapter Three
The Enslaving Power of Debt

"A creditor is worse than a master; for a master owns only your person, a creditor owns your dignity."

-Victor Hugo-

As I opened the mail this morning I noticed a colorful advertisement tucked neatly inside my telephone bill. The ad said I could get a new cordless telephone for just $27.45 per month for a period of four months for a total cost of $109.80. In bold black letters appeared this enticing statement **"no finance charge!"**

As I looked at the ad I wondered how many home owners actually had $109.80 extra cash to buy a new telephone. To many, like myself, this would be a considerable unbudgeted expense. However, it seems that businesses and advertisers are aware of this fact and so they attempt to allure the consumer to buy their product on the "easy monthly installment plan." After all $27.45 a month does not seem as steep as $109.80 and to top it off there's no finance charge.

This reveals just one of the many subtle ways the seller coaxes the buyer into spending money he may or may not possess. A person who purchases any item or service on time or with credit creates an obligation that must be paid at some future time. Today we refer to this as "deficit spending" or the spending of money obtained by borrowing.

Ironically, many Christians refuse to shackle themselves by purchasing a telephone on time, but will not hesitate to subjugate their income, long term, to purchase a home. In the Portland area, where we live, the average price of a home runs about $80,000 (as of Summer, 1990). If the buyer puts $10,000 down and borrows $70,000 for 30 years at 10% interest he will pay $614.00 each month for 360 months. The total amount paid for his $80,000 house is almost three times the purchase price, an awesome $221,151.60.

Our goal in this book centers on saving the reader some or all of this formidable amount. For instance, by adding $4.60 per day or $138.00 each month, the borrower would save $85,750.20 (more than the original amount borrowed) and reduce the length of his loan by 15 years.

Christian Attitudes Concerning Debt

"Credit is not necessarily the same as debt, and life is no longer as physically simplistic as it was when Proverbs was written," writes a Christian financial consultant. [1] The author comments further saying, "but using debt or credit as a tool in a long term cogent financial plan is smart. It is wise and sound financial management." [2]

We disagree that the book of Proverbs is outdated and no longer useful in determining sound economic principles in our day of complexity. Such teaching certainly casts a shadow of doubt on the power of God's Word to transform our thinking on monetary matters.

The Proverb says, "the rich rules over the poor, and the borrower is servant to the lender" (Proverbs 22:7). According to the wisdom of this world and the twentieth century compromising church, the borrower is no longer the unwise slave of his creditor. He is now smart, and exercises good, sound judgment in his financial affairs.

"Do not be deceived, God is not mocked; for whatever a man sows, that he will also reap (Gal 6:7)." If we sow a life of debt we will reap the fruits of living beyond our means. The Proverb says such a reward is servitude. God has called us to remain debt free except in our love to one another (Rom 13:8). The person who borrows finds himself indebted to another man, crippling his freedom to serve Christ.

Those who promote the compromising teaching of Christian debt conclude that "credit (which becomes debt when extended) is an inescapable part of modern life. All of us at one time or another will have to acquire money from an outside source." [3] Is this prophecy true? Are we all condemned to a destiny of debt? If we continually hear this teaching we will undoubtedly believe it. If we instruct our children with this "inescapable debt" mentality they too will accept deficit spending as a necessary part of life. This chapter and the following will attempt to show the danger of this modern day fallacy.

Debt Defined

Debt has been defined in various ways and indeed even among Christians we find disagreement. One Christian economist defines debt as "the inability to meet agreed-upon obligations." According to this definition debt does not occur until the one who buys something on credit violates the terms of the contract. The author says this is the scriptural definition but he fails to include a biblical reference.[4]

Another well know Christian economist defines debt as "any money owed to anyone for anything."[5] This definition seems to coincide with scripture and will be utilized for this study. In Matthew 6:12 sin is viewed as a debt and becomes an obligation at the time of occurrence. When we become Christians we are debtors to live according to the Spirit (Rom 8:12). The apostle Paul was obligated, by debt, to preach the gospel both to the Greeks and the barbarians (Rom 1:14). This was not something that Paul was obliged to do upon failing to meet the terms of some agreement. This debt incurred when God called Paul to preach the gospel.

When a man seeks to justify himself by the works of the law and becomes circumcised he obligates himself to keep the whole law. This "debt" or obligation occurs at the time of circumcision not at the time he may break part of the agreement to keep the whole law (Galatians 5:3). In each of these instances the word "debt" or "debtor" denotes something owed at the time the debt occurs not at the time one fails to meet some part of an agreement or contract.

Debt Enslaves the Borrower

"The servant was not a free man. He was subject to the will and command of his master." 6 When a person borrows money he no longer remains free. He becomes a servant to the lender and sacrifices a portion of his future income. When he receives a loan, the borrower incurs a debt, for which he obligates himself to repay, usually with interest. The Bible refers to this practice of borrowing as servitude or bondage (Pro. 22:7).

Commenting on this verse, Matthew Henry said **"some sell their liberty to gratify their luxury."** 7 Unfortunately, for many Americans the riches of this world mean more than liberty. They fail to remember that religious, political and economic freedom shaped this country from a vast wilderness into a strong nation. Many sacrificed the luxuries of Europe to secure the freedoms of the New World. Today we mortgage our future and freedom to obtain temporary, fleeting pleasures even if we have to borrow the money to obtain them.

The apostle Peter warned against false prophets who would entice the brethren through "the lusts of the flesh" and at the same time promise them liberty. In reality these false prophets were slaves of corruption and when a person is overcome by them he is brought into bondage (II Peter 2:18-19). When allured into luxury at the cost of going into debt, remember that a financial obligation in the form of a loan constitutes bondage. Matthew Poole's insight is helpful regarding Proverbs 22:7. He suggests that "the design of the proverb is partly ...to oblige all men to diligence, whereby they may deliver themselves from this servitude." [8]

The story of Onesimus, in the book of Philemon, provides us with an interesting parallel between slavery and financial bondage. The apostle Paul commends gaining greater freedom to serve Christ.

As many pagans, in Corinth, became Christians they tended to cast off their existing relationships and callings thinking it essential for serving their new LORD. The uncircumcised wanted to become circumcised, the married desired to release their spouses, the single sought marriage partners and slaves longed for their freedom. To curtail this problem, Paul instructed the Corinthians to "remain in the same calling in which they were called" (I Cor 7:17-27).

However, this did not mean that if the LORD provided a change of a persons condition, they were unable to accept that change. To the slave, Paul said, "do not be concerned about it (ie...being a slave); but if you can be made free, rather use it. For he who is called in the LORD while a slave is the LORD'S freedman. Likewise he who is called while free is Christ's slave" (I Cor 7:21-22).

The LORD's freedman actually serves another master and is bound to him as long as required. He cannot serve the LORD with the same ability as the free person. While living as someone's servant, the freedman's labor is owned by his master and the LORD does not obligate him to serve as though free from this earthly obligation. Similarly, the one who is a free man when called into the LORD'S service actually becomes Christ's slave because he has no such earthly entanglement.

Onesimus was a slave who wanted to obtain his freedom from Philemon. The apostle Paul interceded for him requesting that Philemon grant him liberty in order to assist Paul in the ministry. Paul sought his consent in the matter so that any favor he granted would be spontaneous and not forced. The final outcome we do not know. If Philemon refused to grant Onesimus freedom then he would be the LORD'S "freedman," unable to serve Christ with the same capacity as a man without earthly obligations. If Philemon granted Onesimus freedom he would become "Christ's slave," and could serve the LORD unrestrained.

The parallel should be clear. Earthly entanglements restrict our service to God. The person who borrows money becomes servant to the lender. Part of his labor goes to his master in the form of monthly payments and interest. One who borrows may have to forsake a calling until his debts are relinquished. Similarly, he may not be able perform a special task for the LORD simply because his debts restrict his flexibility. In such cases if one can obtain his freedom sooner he should do so for financial freedom means greater liberty to serve Christ. Luke 9:57-62 and Matt 18:21-35 illustrate how worldly entanglements and debt bondage restrict one's freedom to minister in the Lord's work. In some cases debtors have even been sent to prison.

George Whitefield and Debt Bondage

For most of us, the name of George Whitefield has become synonymous with evangelism and open air preaching. Few realize his love for children and attempts to build and operate an orphanage in the wilderness of Georgia. For Whitefield, this "Bethesda" or "House of Mercy" would extend kindness and compassion to homeless and destitute children. It would become a haven where the gospel would influence the lives of neglected youth.

The cost of completing the project was beyond the means of Whitefield. Financial support appeared secure from such sources as the governor, trustees, the Archbishop and Charles Wesley and the Holy Club. In addition, "William Seward took the position of backing the undertaking with his own substance and acted as jointly responsible in its expenses." [9] Whitefield believed further assistance "would be forthcoming from Thomas Noble and others of similar means, and there was no doubt but that he would be able to receive large collections in both Britain and America." [10] In short, Whitefield presumed on the future.

Before long Whitefield faced severe problems. Disagreement arose between him and the Trustees which resulted in the loss of their support. In 1740 the local magistrates began interfering with the management of "Bethesda" causing untold disruption. The same year Spaniards stole supplies bound for the orphanage. The loss from this incident added to the cost of building and maintaining the orphanage "placed him (Whitefield) heavily in debt and he found that he owed the large sum of about 500 pounds sterling (about 20 years wages)." [11]

Moreover, Whitefield soon learned that financial assistance from William Seward, who joined him in support of the endeavor, was no longer forthcoming. During an evangelistic campaign Seward "was struck by a heavy stone from close range." On October 22, 1740 he died without a will leaving Whitefield in sore straits. A distraught Whitefield confessed: "I was embarrassed with Mr. Seward's death. He died without making any provision for me, and I was at the same time much indebted for the Orphan House." [12] In almost total despair Whitefield declared: "I am almost tempted to wish I had never undertaken the Orphan House." [13]

The debt against "Bethesda" became Whitefield's most pressing problem. "Day by day he bore its burden and did so alone. The threat of imprisonment was a constant reality and his enemies gloated in anticipation of seeing it fulfilled." [14] His last source of help rested in his friend Thomas Noble. This hope ended abruptly with the news of Noble's death. To complicate matters Noble left no provision for the orphanage and Whitefield's indebtedness was not forgiven. [15]

In a letter to one of his creditors Whitefield demonstrates the anguish of his bondage. "If possible I shall discharge the debt within six months, but I am afraid it will be out of my power, having met with many disappointments. As we are Brethren of the same Lord, and as the debt was contracted for Him, I hope you will be patient with me." [16] Whitefield knew his responsibility for only "the wicked borrows and does not repay" (Psalm 37:21).

Later "he spoke of the debt as 'lying like a dead weight upon me' and his letters of the ensuing months show him struggling beneath the load,...sick and at times seemingly dying, yet anxious lest by dying in debt he bring reproach on the name of the Lord." [17] In his letters we witness, a tired and beaten Whitefield frequently "expressing his longing 'for the day when I shall owe no man anything but love.'" [18]

Conclusion

In an attempt to relieve his debt, Whitefield later purchased a plantation in South Carolina and utilized slaves for its operation. The funds raised from the venture would reduce his indebtedness on the orphanage. Arnold Dallimore notes that "Whitefield was making himself a partner in the practice of slavery, with all the inhumanity inherent therein."[19]

We should observe how easy it becomes for sin to multiply. Whitefield erred in accumulating debt for which he could not pay and upon his error he added the sin of unlawfully owning human beings against their will.

Whitefield's story does not end on this sad note. Even under a heavy load of debt, he continued to preach the word and labor for the Lord with all his ability. God, after bringing Whitefield through flaming trials caused by his own foolishness, extended His mercy to him.

While in Scotland, in 1768, Whitefield received a legacy of an unknown amount. The funds could be used in any way he saw fit. He spoke of finally paying off all his indebtedness on the Orphanage. [20] " 'The Orpahn House shall have it all,' he exclaimed, and his words ring with a particular sense of delight." [21] "The legacy received in Scotland had not only paid off Bethesda's debt, but also provided a considerable sum in hand." [22]

God desires that we owe no man anything. "The biblical ideal is zero debt (Romans 13:8a). Freedom from debt is a better way of life. People should take it if it is offered to them." [23] Whitefield applied this law when God provided him the resources. He chose to apply the inheritance to his debt instead of spending the money on himself. To get out of bondage many of us will have to work harder and apply all our available cash to clear our debts. The apostle Paul said, "if you can gain your freedom, do so" (I Cor. 7:21). Financial freedom is better than financial bondage.

Chapter Four
Other Hazards of Debt

"Debt is the worst poverty."

-*Thomas Fuller*-

Susanna Wesley gazed upon the three acres of land and the family's new home in Epworth. "This is a wonderful place for our children," she exclaimed. Life for Samuel and Susanna seemed to be improving. Samuel's new position as vicar of St. Andrew's Parish would increase his income from 50 pounds a year to 200 pounds. His poems and books were selling well and he could now farm the land on which the new rectory stood. 1

Soon the Wesleys discovered that additional expenses came with their new responsibilities. Samuel needed extra money to pay for a Broad Seal which the Queen required on certain documents. The government demanded more taxes from clergymen who received promotions. Samuel would now have to pay a First Fruits Tax in the amount of 28 pounds, the John of Jerusalem Tax of 3 pounds and a 3 pound tax for tithes. To complicate matters, Samuel lost income from the sale of his poems when his publisher went out of business. 2

When they moved to Epworth, the Wesleys found that their furniture was inadequate for the new rectory. To acquire these "needed items" plus some farming tools, Samuel borrowed 100 pounds from the local goldsmith who also served as a banker. This loan only increased Samuel's already existing debt load.

Financial troubles continued to escalate when their barn caved in adding 40 pounds repair costs to their bills. Samuel's mother needed help as her creditors would soon take her to debtor's prison. To keep this from happening Samuel took it upon himself to send her 10 pounds annually. [3] Samuel's debts proved a constant worry to Susanna. [4]

Samuel's imprisonment for debt seemed imminent. Each knock at the door brought paralyzing fear to Susanna. Early one morning as he was leaving the church a man approached Samuel and stated, "you're under arrest."

"And for what?" Samuel inquired.

"Debt" replied the man.

Samuel was taken to prison without even saying good-bye to his wife. There he lingered for some three of four months leaving his family in dire need and severely restricting his service for God. [5]

Debt Robs God, Family and the Poor

The prophet Malachi condemned the nation of Israel for robbing the LORD. The Israelites seemed confused for they asked "in what way have we robbed you?" Malachi's response rang loud and clear for all who had ears to hear. The people robbed God "in their tithes and offerings" (Mal 3:8). Today Christians are guilty of the same crime. Estimates indicate that American churchgoers give about 2.5% of their income. [6] God condemned the whole nation of Israel for their robbing him in their tithes and offerings and yet according to Robert Alden "most churches still fall under this indictment; their budgets are generally nowhere near 10 percent of the income of the members." [7]

One common excuse for Christians not giving a full tithe is "we can't afford it." Yet, if we could examine the finances of many who give this excuse we might possibly find a mountain of debt. When Christians sell themselves into deficit spending they rob God of what rightly belongs to Him. Creditors won't wait so the work of the LORD gets put on hold, waiting for the "brighter days ahead."

Another way we rob God is our neglect of the poor. When debt overcomes us we have no extra cash to help the needy around us. God gave explicit instructions for loaning to the destitute and needy. To qualify as a poor person, one's collateral consisted of the cloak on his back. To protect both parties, loans made to anyone with material resources were secured with a pledge. Loaning money, among brethren, existed solely for helping the impoverished and those truly in need and the charging of interest was prohibited (Exodus 22:25-27, Leviticus 25:35-38, Deut 24:10-13).

The LORD enumerated further instructions regarding loans to the poor in Deuteronomy 15:1-11.

At the end of every seven years all debts incurred by the poor were cancelled. This would insure that there would be no poor persons among the Israelites. God intended to bless the nation of Israel in their new land by eliminating the needy by means of loving care, compassion and generosity. Israel would never be a debtor nation but she would loan to many. These blessings prevailed as long as Israel remained faithful and obedient to the LORD.

In the process of eliminating poverty in Israel the Israelites were responsible to help those in need. The LORD declared that "good will come to him who is generous and lends freely" (Psalm 112:5) and "he who is kind to the poor lends to the LORD, and he will reward him for what he has done (Pro. 19:17). Calvin observed that "God...is deprived by us of his right, when we are unkind to the poor, and refuse them aid in their necessity." 8 When we mistreat the poor and become tightfisted in providing for their needs we actually mistreat the LORD. If we are so deep in debt that we cannot give to God His due, then we need to evaluate our priorities and our spending habits and repent, taking the necessary action for change.

Finally, the LORD has given fathers the responsibility to provide for their relatives, and especially for their immediate family (I Tim 5: 8). If debt keeps us from rendering food, clothing and other essential items to our family, then we have denied the faith and are worse than unbelievers. If a brother finds himself in this situation it is imperative that he get out of debt as soon as possible. Some helpful suggestions will be offered in a later chapter of this book.

Debt and Discontentment

"I'll give you Gregg Jeffries and Eric Anthony for your Bo Jackson," cried my youngest son Michael as he waved his baseball cards in my face.
" No!" retorted older brother Daniel."I want dad's Bo Jackson. "Dad," he countered, "I'll give you Todd Zeile and Gary Sheffield for your Bo."
While these two sons continued their efforts, my oldest son, Sam, tried desperately to obtain my Will Clark baseball card.
As the bargaining carried on voices got louder, tempers rose and the loving, respectful spirit we started with began to disappear. Discontentment with the several cards already in their possession began to overcome the boys. Their desire for more and more of their favorite players' cards eventually drove them to ask for an advance on their next allowance.
The lack of contentment causes many people to overspend and even go into debt. The LORD instructs us to keep our lives free from the love of money and to be content with what we have (Heb. 13:5, I Tim 6:6-8). Often times we are led to believe that financial wealth and worldly possessions evidence great gain in our lives. However, the scriptures teach us, "Better is little with the fear of the Lord than great treasure and trouble therewith"(Prov.15:16). "Godliness with contentment is great gain" (I Tim 6:6).
Closely connected with discontentment lies the love of money or mammon. People who desire the things of this world and the riches it provides bring

upon themselves many griefs and sorrows. Some even abandon the faith in pursuit of worldly wealth (I Tim 6:9-10). Because of this insatiable love for money and possessions many fall into grievous debt. "He who loves silver will not be satisfied with silver; nor he who loves abundance, with increase" (Ecc.5:10 NKJV). The discontented person will never be satisfied. He will resort to deficit spending in order to gain the abundance he desires.

In his commentary on the book of Hebrews, John MacArthur offers Christians six ways of reaching contentment. First, "we must realize God's goodness." [9] Romans 8:28 declares "that all things work together for good to those who love God, to those who are the called according to His purpose." At first we may not understand why we might be experiencing financial difficulties but we must trust God to work them out for our good as He promised. To go into debt when we already lack the cash to purchase the item interferes with God's providing goodness. Listen to Moses as he spoke to the children of Israel when Pharaoh and his army approached them. "Stand still and see the salvation of the LORD" he cried (Ex 14:13). The same God that saved the Israelites from this awesome foe can surely save us from financial woes.

Second, "we should realize... that God is omniscient." [10] We must take confidence in Christ who said "do not worry, saying, what shall we eat? or what shall we drink? or what shall we wear?...your heavenly father knows that you need them. But seek first his kingdom and his righteousness, and all these things will be given to you as well" (Matt 6:31-33). If we believe that God knows our needs and will meet them and if we live by the standards of His kingdom we won't have to become a servant to the lender.

Third, "we should think about what we deserve." 11 In days past, before our conversion, we were all children of wrath deserving the judgment of God. But God, who is rich in mercy, saved us by His grace (unmerited favor). Like the centurion in Luke 7:6, we do not deserve to have the LORD come into our presence and we are not worthy to go to Him. Any blessings we have come by His grace for He richly provides us with everything for our enjoyment (I Tim 6:17).

While preaching the gospel among the Gentiles in Lystra, the apostle Paul declared that even the undeserving heathen nations receive God's grace. Just as the crowd attempted to offer sacrifice to Paul and Barnabas, Paul urged them to repent from their idolatry and worship the one true God who had shown them kindness by giving them rain and crops in their seasons and plenty of food to eat filling their hearts with joy (Acts 14:8-20).

If we stop to think how unworthy we are of His goodness and blessings, we should be content with what He has given us. This contentment would supply the needed power to resist the temptation of obtaining additional goods with money He has not yet, in His goodness, provided.

Fourth, "we should recognize God's supremacy, His sovereignty." 12 It is the LORD who gives the ability for gaining prosperity (Deut 8:18) and He is the one who sends poverty and wealth (I Sam 2:7). If we find ourselves lacking in material things we must receive it as the LORD'S sovereign will and wait on Him to provide in His time and good pleasure.

Remember, He works out everything in conformity with the purpose of His will (Eph 1:11). If we wait on God's timing there will be no need to accumulate debt.

Fifth, "we should continually remind ourselves what true riches are." [13] The riches of Christ are unsearchable (Eph 3:8). A wealthy young man was instructed to sell his possessions that he might obtain heavenly treasures (Mark 10:21) and the LORD instructed His followers to store up treasures in heaven and not on earth (Matt 6:19-21).

Since our citizenship is in heaven (Phil 2:20) we should set our minds on the things above not on the things of this world (Col 3:2). If we are heavenly minded we won't be concerned about worldly wealth that perishes. Our lives will be free from the love of money and we will avoid going into debt to obtain earthly riches.

Finally, we must realize that "contentment comes from communion with God." [14] The LORD taught us the impossibility of serving two masters. The reason is obvious. Eventually we will learn to love one master above the other and become devoted to him. We cannot serve both God and mammon (riches) for the two are in opposition (Matt 6:24). True devotion to God will avoid the entanglements of worldly riches. The warnings God gives to the rich in the Bible are clear.

The wealthy find it difficult to enter the kingdom of God and commonly put their hope in the riches they accumulate (Matt 19:16-23). Often they struggle to do good deeds and frequently are unwilling to share (Luke 16:19-31). Most annoying is the tendency for the rich to oppress the poor even in the church (James 2:1-7). Some will not think twice to loan their money to the poor at interest (usury), a practice condemned in scripture by the LORD. Truly, if we are communing with God, the riches of the world will become less attractive and desirable and we will learn to be content with what we have, avoiding the snare of falling into debt.

Debt and Greed

Born in 1734, Robert Morris "apprenticed his way into business until he became one of the wealthiest men in America." [15] His "mercantile genius earned huge profits, which he reinvested in ships and goods to make more profits. He engaged in banking, money exchange, imports, exports, and shipping, the normal pursuits...of that era." [16] Some considered him "the merchant prince of Philadelphia." [17] He is best known as "the financier of the Revolution." [18]

Finances during the war were slim and Congress had very little credit. Without the personal integrity and funds of men like Robert Morris the Continental cause was futile. In New Jersey, General Washington survived a winter campaign only with the help of Robert Morris. He "secured the money that supplied the Army on the Delaware, and permitted

Washington to capture Trenton." [19] Later Morris pledged a personal note and his honor to obtain funds needed for Washington to claim victory at Princeton.[20]

After the new nation was established in 1787 Robert Morris, motivated by optimism and greed, began to speculate heavily in Western lands. To secure these properties Morris borrowed large sums of money. He eventually controlled some 6 million acres in Pennsylvania alone. [21]

In the late 1790's depression hit the colonies and brought financial ruin to Morris's estate. He owed his creditors some $3 million which he could not pay. In 1797 Morris declared bankruptcy and ended up in debtor's prison. When released in 1801, "Robert Morris was a broken man." [22] He died in poverty in 1806. [23]

The LORD Jesus warned, "Watch out! Be on your guard against all kinds of greed; a man's life does not consist in the abundance of his possessions" (Luke 12:15). "So disastrous is it that the last of the Ten Commandments prohibits it (covetousness), the only prohibition in the second table that concerns an attitude rather than an action." [24]

In his day, Charles Spurgeon complained that "the acts of many of Christ's followers have been the cause of justifying and comforting sinners in their evil ways.... The covetousness of too many Christians has had this effect." He went to ask, "How often has it happened that some of you have bent your knee in the sanctuary, and have said, 'Forgive us our debts, as we forgive our debtors,' and one hour afterwards your finger has been almost meeting your thumb through the jugular vein of some debtor whom you had seized by the throat?" [25]

Covetousness or greed has been defined as "the desire to have more." [26] When Achan saw the spoils of Jericho he coveted them and took them against the LORD'S command. As a result he and his entire family were put to death (Joshua 7). Likewise greed has been the downfall of many Christians. Having gazed upon and coveted the riches of others, Christians have amassed for themselves a mound of debt. The example they set before the world has a similar effect upon sinners as that which Spurgeon denounced in his day. Other Christians have stumbled into greed and debt by following the example of their brothers and sisters.

Larry Burkett confesses "I often hear young married couples' discussions about their start on the road to indebtedness. They simply followed the example of other people who borrowed to get the things they wanted--furniture, new cars, televisions, and such." [27] "Watch out! Be on your guard against all kinds of greed." Covetousness just might lead you into financial bondage.

Debt and Presumption

In 1634 a peculiar rage hit the states of Germany and Holland. Tulips became the modern status symbol of both the rich and the middle class. It is reported that a single bulb could sell for 6,000 Dutch florins, which in modern American terms means

$22,000. One trader supposedly paid half of his fortune for a single root while another gave up his new carriage, two horses, and a complete set of harness for one single bulb.

"Everyone imagined that the passion for tulips would last forever.... Many people sold or mortgaged their houses and farms just to purchase the bulbs.... The tulip traders thought prices would rise forever.... Finally the structure collapsed.... The market value of the Semper Augustus bulb plunged from 6,000 florins to 500 florins-a 91 percent drop." [28]

Many people today believe that borrowing money for appreciating items is both wise and good. Any one who borrows with this notion presumes on the future. However, as the above story dramatically illustrates, things do not appreciate forever. Whenever my wife and I visit our friends in the San Francisco Bay Area, we find it amazing how much they pay for homes and property. The values keep escalating and many fear what the future holds. Some want to get out while they can. In all likelihood the structure will collapse.

The proverb says "do not boast about tomorrow, for you do not know what a day may bring forth" (Pro 27:1). How many people borrow money expecting things to remain the same? Later they may become sick or lose their job and find themselves unable to make their loan payment. F. Delitzsch notes "this boasting is foolish and presumptuous, for the future is God's; not a moment of the future is in our own power."[29]

James gives us some sound advice concerning

our actions in the future. "Now listen, you who say, 'today or tomorrow we will go to this or that city, spend a year there, carry on business and make money.' Why you do not even know what will happen tomorrow. What is your life? You are a mist that appears for a little while and then vanishes. Instead you ought to say, 'if it is the Lord's will, we will live and do this or that' (Ja 4:13-15). Matthew Henry notes "we are cautioned against a presumptuous confidence of the continuance of our lives, and against forming projects thereupon with assurance of success." [30]

The two most prominent Christian financial advisors today seem reluctant to call any type of borrowing sin. Ron Blue comments, "the Bible does not say it's a sin to borrow money" but it "does give many warnings about being in debt." Furthermore he states "it doesn't say you are out of God's will or have violated a commandment when you borrow." [31] He concludes that "from a biblical perspective, we are free to borrow money, but there are consequences we must bear when we do." [32]

Similarly, Larry Burkett teaches that "principles of borrowing appear in God's Word, although it needs to be remembered that these are principles, not laws....A principle is an instruction from the Lord to help guide our decisions. A law is an absolute. Negative consequences may follow from ignoring a principle, but punishment is the likely consequence of ignoring a law God has given us." [33]

Although these highly qualified advisors say it's not wrong or sinful to borrow, they contradict themselves when they teach that "it's wrong to presume upon the future." Ron Blue remarks, "presuming upon the future to borrow money violates not only a caution, but also a command" and resolves that "all debt presumes upon the future unless there is a guaranteed (fully collateralized) way to repay." [34]

It seems to me that if something violates a command we can determine that it is sin. Obviously, not all debt is sin, however any debt incurred apart from the biblical principles of desperation and need would constitute a violation of God's laws. Loans granted on the basis of the borrower's need to survive do not presume on the future. Similarly, loans to the needy backed with pledges (collateral) insure against the debtor's inability to repay his obligation and do not constitute presumption (Exodus 22:25-27, Leviticus 25:35-38, Deut 24:10-13). For the lender, such loans are to be considered as gifts (Luke 6:34-36).

When borrowing with a pledge, such as in the purchase of real estate, the property becomes the collateral and normally can be returned in case of default. However, in most states, when a borrower defaults on a home mortgage, the lender can sue to recover his loss. The asset itself acts as a guarantee to repay a loan only when its marketable value exceeds the current loan balance. Most defaults occur during economic bad times, when property values decline.

Finally, Ron Blue believes that using a credit card for convenience, knowing you have the money in the bank to pay the bill when it comes due, "does not presume upon the future." [35] This type of controlled use of your credit card does not constitute sin.

Borrowing money on the notion that we will be alive and healthy tomorrow while still maintaining our present employment establishes a false claim upon God's goodness and providence. Since most borrowing presumes upon the future, we conclude that most debt is sin. The exceptions noted in the Bible for the poor and destitute (Lev 25:35-38) and those needy persons who guarantee their debt with collateral (Deut 24:10-13, Ez 18:7,12) constitute the exceptions. Frequently the value of one's pledge depreciates and no longer covers the outstanding balance. Loans of this type should be conducted with great precaution. Debt should be avoided to the best of our power and ability.

Conclusion

The Christian must give attention to Paul's injunction to "owe no man anything" (Rom 13:8). Wuest suggests that this command "forbids the continuance of an action already going on" and can be translated "stop owing to anyone even one thing... Pay your debts." [36]

Having shown the Roman believers the necessity of giving to everyone what is owed, including the payment of taxes to the civil magistrate, Paul proceeds to instruct them to have no unpaid debts. John Murray notes that to "owe no man anything " must be taken as imperative and "does condemn the looseness with which we contract debts and particularly the indifference so often displayed in the discharging of them." He goes on do say that "few things bring greater reproach upon the Christian profession than the accumulation of debts and refusal to pay them." [37]

Borrowing by believers other than the poor gives the world a distorted view of the Christian God. Christians often boast that "my God will meet all my needs according to his glorious riches in Christ Jesus" (Phil 4:19). When one makes this claim and then runs to the local bank to borrow money at usury he sends a conflicting message to the world. Either God will take care of our needs or the nearest moneylender will. As Christians, we need to consider the kind of testimony we impart with every action we make. In everything we do we must ask, Will it glorify God or will it destroy his reputation?

In this chapter we have discussed what constitutes debt, and examined some of its dangers. The Bible teaches us that borrowing money enslaves the borrower, robs God of His just tithes and offerings, cheats the family of their daily necessities and takes from the poor what should be given to them to sustain life. Borrowing also leads to discontentment, greed and presumption. In the next section we will discuss the history and morality of usury.

Chapter Five
The History of Usury: Part One
Ancient Times to Christ

"Interest works night and day, in fair weather and in foul. It gnaws at a man's substance with invisible teeth."

-Henry Ward Beecher-

Death loomed heavily in the colony that first winter of 1621. Before slipping into spring it claimed the lives of nearly half of the plantation's small population. Later that same year the Fortune arrived with thirty five additional colonists but no extra food and supplies. To complicate matters, Thomas Weston, the London merchant who helped finance their voyage, sent along a large letter "full of complaints and expostulations about former passages at Hampton, and the keeping the ship (Mayflower) so long in the country, and returning her without lading (cargo or freight to pay their debt)." [1]

The letter also included pointed accusations against the Pilgrims as to the reasons why they made no attempt to make a payment on their obligation. He further instructed them to supply him with an accounting of their expenditures and encouraged them to send the ship back with plenty of merchandise to sell. [2]

At this time, Robert Cushman, the financial advisor of the colony, convinced the Pilgrims to sign a revised agreement with Weston. They reasoned that not agreeing to the new conditions "would close their last channel for desperately needed supplies, and they would be totally cut off." [3] This new agreement would keep the Pilgrims in bondage for twenty years, sometimes paying as high as 30 to 50 percent interest on borrowed money. In addition, "it took some twenty thousand pounds to retire a debt of eighteen hundred."[4]

To accomplish this William Bradford sold a large farm, John Alden and Miles Standish, three hundred acres each and Edward Winslow and Thomas Prence, their homes. [5] The Pilgrims learned the hard way that debt with usury equals extended servitude. In this chapter we want to examine the history and nature of usury.

Definition of Terms

Throughout the centuries philosophers, economists and businessmen have grappled with the problem of usury or the charging of interest on the purchase or use of wealth. Generally the debate revolves around two basic questions; 1) Why does usury exist? and; 2) Is usury morally right? In this chapter we will attempt to supply an answer to these questions. The reader should note this is **an** answer and does not profess to be **the** answer or final word on the subject.

For the reader's benefit definitions of some key terms are supplied. Wealth is defined as "man-produced goods that have value." [6] Normally, economists classify wealth into two categories. The first consists of capital goods or "goods destined for the acquisition of further goods." [7] These may include such items as tools, equipment and machinery. The second is composed of consumer goods or goods used "for the direct satisfaction of human wants." [8] These may contain such things as stereos, television sets, jewelry and furniture.

Usury, or interest, is commonly defined as a "factor payment made for the use of wealth."[9] In the following discussion wealth will be limited to the use of money because it is the normal means by which we acquire goods and pay our debts. Money has been defined as "a commodity used to facilitate trade... or a medium of exchange." [10] The reader should keep in mind that money, such as we use today, possesses no intrinsic value. The only worth it contains consists of government fiat.

The History of Usury in Israel

The people of Israel stood alone among the nations in its laws and customs. The "gentiles" worshipped many gods while the Israelites praised only the God of their father Abraham. Common practice among the heathen included unconcern for the poor. Those who loaned money demanded more than the amount borrowed in return (usury) and often times required the borrower to secure his loan with personal property which might include himself and his family. The Israelites owned no such practice! [11]

On Mount Sinai, the LORD delivered to Moses instructions that would govern His people concerning borrowing and lending. These laws would later be read to the children of Israel just before entering the land of Canaan. God's precepts restricted the loaning of wealth to the poor and needy and denied the lender the right to charge them interest. Loans to foreigners at interest were permitted.

Any garment taken in pledge from the destitute borrower was returned before sundown because it was his only covering to protect him while he slept at night. Any loan made to a needy, but not necessarily destitute, person was to be secured with a pledge at the time of contracting the agreement. This protected the creditor from loss and the debtor from extended financial bondage should he be unable to repay the loan. The pledge was returned to the borrower after he fulfilled his obligation (Deut 24:10-13, Ez 18:7,12). Normally, to qualify for a loan in Israel one's condition consisted of desperation (Ex 22:25-27). The Bible records no incident nor any instruction for borrowing by those without need.

In addition, the more fortunate carried the responsibility of helping those who became poor in Israel. They should not refuse the needy but care for them as a guest or alien resident. To the Hebrews, charging interest to a brother was like "biting" him for the Hebrew words "*nashak* and *neshek*" mean "to strike with a sting (as a serpent)." [12] Furthermore, the Israelites were prohibited from taking any other form of "increase" or "profit" on money, food or anything else loaned to the destitute so that they could live together in the land (Lev 25:35-38, Deut 23:19).

Loans to strangers constituted the only exception to the usury laws. The LORD declared, "to a foreigner you may charge interest" (Deut 23:20). The word translated "foreigner" comes from "*nokree*" and is used negatively in the sense of something adulterous or outlandish. [13] "This could have been a traveller or foreigner who owned a business locally. It could have been a business contact in another country." [14]

As an unbeliever and enemy of God, the "outlandish stranger" could be subjected to financial bondage. He was not to receive mercy like a brother or a gentile sojourner who chose to live among the Israelites and worship their God (Ex 20:21, Lev 25:35). Perhaps the LORD would use financial pressure to bring the foreigner to repent and worship the one true God. As one commentator notes, the taking of interest "was a means of subduing him, his family, and his God-defying civilization. It was (and is) a means of dominion." [15]

God's mercy extended one step beyond the heathen nations. Every seventh year all debts were cancelled and every creditor released his neighbor of his obligation. The seventh year release did not apply to the foreigner who was still required to pay his loan. Ideally and theoretically the obeying of this law would rid the land of poverty, but because of disobedience, the poor would never cease from the land (Deut 15:1-11).

In Psalm 15 David asked the LORD, "Who may abide in your tabernacle? Who may dwell in your holy hill? Part of the answer lies in how one uses his money. The man who does not charge usury for the use of his wealth finds favor with God and will never be moved (vs.5). On the other hand the "one who increases his possessions by usury" will end up giving it up to someone "who will pity the poor" (Pro 28:8). In judging the nation of Israel the LORD declared, through the prophet Ezekiel, life to those who did not exact usury or take any form of increase and death to those who did (Ez 18:4-13).

After returning to Israel after the Babylonian captivity, the Jews incurred financial difficulties. They had no food to eat, their lands and vineyards were mortgaged, some borrowed money to pay the king's tax and their sons and daughters were driven to slavery. After hearing of this news, Nehemiah became angry and rebuked the nobles and rulers saying "each of you is exacting usury from his brother." Their condemnation was clear and just and they agreed to restore everything to its rightful owner according to the law, including the "hundredth part" (one percent) charged as usury (Neh 5:1-13).

God intended to bless his people and keep them from every kind of bondage. They would lend to many nations but they would never borrow. They would rule over many nations but not be ruled by them. They would be the head and not the tail. Financial bondage is never God's plan for His people.

The History of Usury in the Ancient World

In answer to the question, "Why are people willing to pay interest?, Tom Rose offers a simple but honest answer. He believes that people who borrow at interest "are in a hurry. They don't like to wait. People would rather consume today than at some time in the future. They are oriented to now!" [16]

In the Ancient World people were no different from today in their attitude on borrowing money at interest. However, just as in our own time, the Ancient World owned its prophets and philosophers who denounced the practice of usury. Among them were Plato, Aristotle, the two Catos, Cicero, Seneca, Plautus and others. [17]

The more pronounced arguments against usury came from Plato and Aristotle. Plato (427 B.C.) scolded usurers as men "intent upon their own business... planting their own stings into any fresh victim who offers them an opening to inject the poison of their money, and while they multiply their capital by usury, they are also multiplying the drones and the paupers." [18] To Plato, usury led to increased poverty and despair.

Later, Aristotle (384 B.C), a student of Plato, carried on the debate against the practice of usury. He stated, "very much disliked also is the practice of charging interest; and the dislike is fully justified, for the gain arises out of currency itself, not as a product of that for which currency was provided. Currency was intended to be a means of exchange, whereas interest represents an increase in the currency itself. Hence its name, (*tokos* meaning offspring), for each animal produces its like, and interest is currency born of currency. And so of all types of business this is the most contrary to nature." [19]

Bohm-Bawerk sums up Aristotle's theory in these words. "Money is by nature incapable of bearing fruit. The lender's gain therefore cannot come from any economic power inherent in money, but only from a defrauding of the borrower. Interest is therefore a gain got by abuse and injustice." [20] The weakness in Aristotle's theory existed in its foundation. His arguments developed from science and pragmatism rather than law. This can be understood by observing the practice of ancient Greece and Rome.

Philosophically and theoretically, interest received condemnation in the ancient world. However, in practice, "moneylending was an old business... and the Aristotelian prohibition was so easily evaded.... Usury (above twelve percent, the legal minimum rate in those days) was widespread, and debtors had periodically to be rescued from their accumulating obligations by bankruptcy or legislation." [21] During the period of the Greek conquest bankers "proliferated and prospered" and fattened themselves "on such relentless usury that cutthroat and moneylender became one word." [22]

After the Roman armies conquered the provinces of Greece, the publicans exacted twice the taxes demanded (half to keep for themselves) to support the new Roman state. If a province could not pay the exorbitant taxes, "Roman financiers would lend them the necessary funds at from 12 to 48 percent interest, to be collected, if need be, by the Roman army." [23] By 70 B.C. the interest debt on these loans soared to six times the principal amount. "To meet the charges on this debt communities sold their public buildings and statuary, and parents sold their children into slavery, for defaulting debtors could be stretched on the rack."[24]

Christ and Usury

The Lord Jesus appeared on the scene during these days of excessive taxes, fraudulent tax gatherers, selfish moneylenders and oppressively preposterous usury rates. The Jews of this era commonly taught the legality of personal retaliation using the law of "an eye for an eye and a tooth for a tooth" to justify their teaching. In reality this law was given to civil government as a limit to the punishment it could inflict upon lawbreakers. It was not intended for citizens to use as a justification for personal vengeance.

Regarding personal offenses, the Lord Jesus' teaching illumined the true intent of the law. If your enemy treats you with harm and evil, return that evil with good. Turn the other cheek. Give up your cloak. Go the extra mile. Give to him who asks. Lend to him who wants to borrow.

A common teaching of the day gave license for the wealthy to refuse the poor and needy. The Lord Jesus corrected this form of retaliation and misuse of the law by saying "give to him who asks you, and from him who wants to borrow from you do not turn away" (Matt 5:38-42). Further light on this subject appears in Luke 6:34 where we read "and if you lend to those from whom you hope to receive back, what credit is that to you? For even sinners lend to sinners to receive as much back."

Upon examining these verses we must keep in mind that their meaning will be consistent with God's teaching in the law of Moses. Therefore the Lord's intention is not for Christians to indiscriminately give away their wealth. As we have seen, in Israel under the law only the needy and destitute borrowed from their neighbor and it was morally wrong to refuse such a brother if you were capable of meeting his need. Likewise under Our Lord's teaching, whenever a truly impoverished or needy person asks for help or a loan, he is not to be refused.

When we lend under these circumstances we do so "hoping for nothing in return" (Luke 6:35). These words apply to the principal amount loaned. Obviously, if we lend without expecting to receive back the original amount we likewise will forego any interest or gain from the transaction. The Christian's attitude toward the poor should be one of generosity. Even though the lender is entitled to receive back his principal he should be willing to dispense with it for the sake of the poor. Notice, to the one who follows these instructions, the LORD says "your reward will be great, and you will be sons of the Highest" (Luke 6:35). No where do we find Our Lord promoting the payment of interest by the poor on loans secured for their assistance. Similarly the rich are never encouraged to borrow, but then why should the rich borrow? This is in full agreement with the law (Ex 22:25-27, Lev 25:35-38, Deut 15:1-11,23:19-20,24:10-13).

Regarding the character of Christianity and its attitude toward usury, Bohm-Bawerk comments "the exploitation of poor debtors by rich creditors must have appeared in a peculiarly hateful light to one whose religion taught him to look upon gentleness and charity as among the greatest virtues, and to think little of the goods of this world." Considering the verses in Luke's gospel above, Bohm-Bawerk notes, "what had most influence (against usury) was that, in the sacred writings of the New Testament, certain passages... seemed to contain a direct divine prohibition of the taking of interest." [25]

A common defense for the practice of usury among Christians appears in Matt 25:27. In dealing with the wicked, lazy servant, his lord said "therefore you ought to have deposited my money with the bankers, and at my coming I would have received back my own with interest." In discussing any parable it is good to keep in mind the intent of the story and not try to find a parallel meaning from contemporary life.

Alfred Edersheim notes that reference here is "the personal work of the disciples... as the servants who are to give an account of their stewardship." [26] The obvious teaching in this passage concerns the "kingdom of heaven" and the return of Christ. It is not a discourse on money management nor is the LORD instructing His followers on how to make wise investments with their money. Furthermore the parable is not intended as a discourse on the morality of usury. The LORD's focus rests on the wise use of earthly wealth to promote the kingdom of heaven so that when Christ returns we may "enter into the joy of our Lord."

"Because the parable illustrates the kingdom of heaven, the man in the story obviously represents Christ Himself, and the going on a journey represents the time He is away from earth between His first and second advents. The slaves depict professed believers...whom He has entrusted with various resources to use in His behalf until He returns." [27]

By His "common grace" the LORD gives every human being certain abilities and riches. Some receive more (5 talents) than others (2 or 1 talent) but all are required to use their gifts in a way pleasing to the gracious giver of such blessings and according to his personal qualifications. In the parable "the responsibilities were given to each according to his own ability. The owner knew his slaves intimately, and he entrusted each one only with the responsibility he reasonably could be expected to handle." [28]

As Christians we are to use these assets to further the work of our Master until He returns. True believers put their resources to work and gain additional riches for their Lord. False professors hoard their wealth and refuse to work diligently for their Master resulting in their condemnation. Edersheim states: "But the great lesson intended is, that every good and faithful servant of Christ must, whatever his circumstances, personally and directly use such talent as he may have to make gain for Christ." [29]

When reading the story of the talents, one may ask of the lawfulness of depositing our money into a bank so as to earn interest. Does Our Lord condone the practice of usury by making such a statement in the parable? The writer believes that banks can serve a legitimate function today as they did in the time of Christ. However, it would be ludicrous to think that Jesus would have condoned any practice, provided by bankers, beyond the restrictions that God established in the Law.

Edersheim notes that the bankers of that day "undertook to make payments, to collect moneys and accounts, to place out money at interest--in short, all the ordinary business of this kind." He goes on to say "there can be no question that the Jewish bankers of Palestine and elsewhere were engaged in the same undertakings." 30 By participating in such business were Jewish bankers exempt from God's law regarding the practice of usury?

Any Jew functioning as a banker remained obligated to refrain from charging interest to his fellow Israelites in need of help. However, he was free to take interest from a foreigner. Interest was legal but constrained to the limits of Biblical Law. Jews could place their money on deposit and gain a return on their money but the banker was forbidden to take advantage of his poor brother by lending him money at interest.

Jewish bankers could charge fees to the wealthy for services rendered, take collateral on loans to needy borrowers who were not desperate and receive interest from foreigners, but they could not oppress the destitute and needy with usury. Jews loaning their money to Roman bankers could lawfully charge them interest for the use of their wealth as Romans were considered foreigners.

The Jewish historian, Josephus, writing during the times of Christ, exhorts his kinsmen to "let no one lend to anyone of the Hebrews upon usury, neither usury of what is eaten or what is drunken; for it is not just to make advantage of the misfortunes of one of thy own countrymen: but when thou hast been assisted to his necessities, think it thy gain, if thou obtainest their gratitude to thee, and withal that reward which will come to thee from God for thy humanity towards him." [31]

Among the various trades in Palestine in the times of Christ, usurers were classified with gamblers and those who organized games of chance. Many viewed them as "notorious tricksters" and their vocations were banned de jure (according to law). [32] They were hated and despised among the people. In Jewish society usurers were ostracized and could never be a judge nor a witness in a court of law. They were deprived of civil and political rights afforded every Israelite. [33]

Jews looked upon any kind of speculation as akin to usury. Creditors were forbidden to use anything belonging to a debtor without paying for its use. "So punctilious were the Rabbis in avoiding the appearance of usury, that a woman who borrowed a loaf from her neighbor was told to fix its value at the time, lest a sudden rise in flour should make the loaf returned worth more than that borrowed." [34]

Considering these facts the words of the Lord Jesus seem astounding. Why would He instruct someone to deposit money with the bankers (Matt. 25:27) who would turn around and loan the money at interest? When we consider the context, Jesus' direction does not seem strange. The importance of obeying the Master and producing fruit for the furthering of His kingdom should be every person's utmost objective in life. The one who buries his talent and produces nothing for his Lord obviously does not believe in Him. He is danger of eternal damnation! When the Master returns to judge every man according to his works those who have neglected their responsibility will be found guilty. They will be cast into outer darkness where there is weeping and gnashing of teeth. Certainly it would be better to put your resources on deposit with the local banker and receive a return for the Master than to be cast into hell forever. By using this illustration in the parable the Lord is stressing the importance of heavenly wealth.

To summarize, the Lord Jesus taught his disciples to loan their wealth to the poor without expecting to receive anything back, including the principal. This teaching precludes them from exacting interest and taking advantage of the unfortunate circumstances of their poor brethren. Loans were intended for those in need and the rich were never instructed to borrow money. The purpose of earthly wealth is for promoting the kingdom of God, including the meeting of personal and familial needs and preparing God's people for the coming of Christ. Banking serves a place in kingdom activities. Moneylenders operate under the moral teachings of God's law when they loan money at interest according to His precepts.

Should the Rich Borrow Money?

Since the Bible gives no instruction for the wealthy to borrow one might ask if it is ever lawful for such a practice. The Scriptures examined above indicate that all references to usury pertained to the poor and needy because they alone were expected to borrow. Should the rich borrow for business or investment purposes? If the Bible is silent regarding such a phenomenon as borrowing by the rich can we conclude that such borrowing is lawful?

The Bible does seem to forbid such a practice and we must conclude that its warnings against debt apply to the rich as well as to the poor. The borrower is always servant to the lender. Presuming on the future is sin. Furthermore, those who borrow without need fall outside the protection of God's law against usury and the cancellation of debt every seventh year. The rich are expected to pay interest and to bear the burden of their debt until paid in full regardless of the length of the loan.

When the rich borrow they make themselves like a foreigner or someone outside of the family of God. In a sense they are saying they want to be treated like one of God's enemies. In addition they subject themselves to financial bondage and are treated as an outlandish stranger. Borrowing is a sign of servitude and being dominated by another. God never intends for His people to experience such bondage. Christians should be the head not the tail.

The rich can become poor by going into debt and mortgaging their wealth. In the case of a defaulting debtor his possessions become property of his creditors. "Better is a little with the fear of the LORD, than great treasure with trouble" (Pro.15:16).

When loaning to the rich, lenders expect compensation for the loss of present goods. The risk of loaning money that will not be repaid causes lenders to require factor payments to cover such losses. Finally, inflation (the increase of the money supply) devalues the monetary unit (the dollar) forcing lenders to charge a premium for the use of their money. The rich borrower should not expect to get something for nothing. There is no such thing as a free lunch.

Conclusion

Like the Pilgrims, many Americans learn the hard way that debt with interest extends the borrowers financial bondage considerably. Usury exists because of covetousness, greed and impatience.

Unlike the nations around them, Israel stood apart as a people with compassion for the poor and destitute. God's law gave His people specific instructions on lending and usury. The rich were not to withhold from the needy and the exacting of usury was prohibited. Every seventh year all outstanding debts were cancelled and God promised blessing to all who extended generosity to the poor.

For the Jews, charging interest was like biting your brother with the strike of a serpent. God permitted Israel to charge interest to foreigners as a form of dominion over them in order that they might repent from their wicked ways and worship the one true God.

Loans were never made to the rich for God reserved this favor for the needy. If the rich insist on borrowing against the clear warnings of Scripture they are to be treated as foreigners. In such cases the borrower should pay interest.

Throughout history the practice of usury received condemnation. In the ancient world spokesmen against usury included Plato and Aristotle. Though denounced by the philosophers, the nefarious custom continued.

Christ never advocated the taking of interest thus affirming the law of Moses. The Lord Jesus explained the intent of the law when he instructed His followers to lend "hoping for nothing in return." The Christian should be generous with the poor for Christ promised a great reward for all who obeyed His instructions.

Chapter Six
The History of Usury: Part Two
The Early Church to Modern Times

"There is one bit of advice given to us by the ancient heathen Greeks, and by the Jews in the Old Testament, and by the great Christian teachers of the Middle Ages, which the modern economic system has completely disobeyed. All these people told us not to lend money at interest."

-*C.S. Lewis*-

When Charles Spurgeon was a young boy he was in the habit of losing his pencils. On one such occasion Charles found himself wanting a stick of slate pencil but he had no money. He sometimes witnessed boys and girls buying nuts and cakes from Mrs. Pearson on credit and soon reasoned that he too could purchase his pencil now and pay for it later.

"Christmas was coming, and somebody or other would be sure to give me a penny then, and perhaps even a whole silver sixpence," he determined. With that he decided to go into debt. Charles gathered his courage and went into the shop to buy his needed pencil. One farthing was the cost and because he had never owed anything before his credit was good. He bought his pencil. He was now in debt for the very first time!

Young Charles's decision pleased him very little. He notes, "I felt as if I had done wrong, but I little knew how soon I should smart for it." Before long his father found him out and Charles experienced the discipline and admonition of the Lord. Regarding this godly correction Charles wrote, "God bless him for it...he did not intend to bring up his children to speculate, and play at what big rogues call financing, and therefore he knocked my getting into debt on the head at once and no mistake. He gave me a very powerful lecture upon getting into debt, and how like it was to stealing, and upon the way in which people were ruined by it, and how a boy who would owe a farthing, might one day owe a hundred pounds, and get into prison, and bring his family into disgrace."

Then young Spurgeon was marched off to the shop. He confessed he felt like a deserter being marched into the barracks. He experienced great shame because he thought everyone knew he was in debt. Upon arrival at the little store "the farthing was paid amid many solemn warnings, and the poor debtor was set free, like a bird let out of a cage." Elated, Charles exclaimed, "how sweet it felt to be out of debt!" He vowed never to get into debt again.

Spurgeon's admonition in later years is good sound advice and worth every father's consideration. It is quoted here in detail.

"If all boys were inoculated with the same doctrine when they were young, it would be as good as a fortune to them, and save them waggon-loads of trouble in after life. God bless my father, say I, and send a breed of such fathers into old England to save her from being eaten up with villainy, for what with companies, and schemes, and paper-money, the nation is getting to be as rotten as touchwood! Ever since that early sickening, I have hated debt as Luther hated the Pope." 1

How desperately we need fathers today who will instruct their sons on the dangers of debt and usury. Our prayer should be that God would send a host of fathers into America to save her from being eaten up with debt, interest, inflation (paper money and credit expansion) and unsound, dishonest monetary policy. America is getting as decayed as dry rot. We must learn and teach our children to hate personal debt and interest as much as the early church fathers.

Usury and the Early Church

In the days immediately following Our Lord's resurrection "all the believers were one in heart and mind. No one claimed that any of his possessions was his own but they shared everything they had" (Acts 4:32). This is not an example of modern communism for these Christians were giving freely from the heart not by enforced government legislation. To these early Christians, the truth of the resurrection was exemplified in their generosity towards the poor.

As a result of these generous acts displayed by the early believers "there were no needy persons among them." The Bible says that this liberal spirit of compassion for the poor extended to the point where "from time to time those who owned lands or houses sold them, brought the money from the sales and put it at the apostles' feet, and it was distributed to anyone as he had <u>need</u>" (Acts 4:34-35). It would seem from these scriptures that the early church understood Our Lord's instruction to lend to those in <u>need</u> without expecting to receive anything in return. To the writer's knowledge, there is absolutely no hint of usury in the economic practices of the first century church.

<u>Tertullian and Latin Christianity</u>

The tradition of the first century church regarding usury passed on to the second and third centuries largely through the writings of Tertullian (A.D. 145-220). In A.D. 207 Tertullian wrote <u>The Five Books Against Marcion,</u> a heretic who believed that the God of the Old Testament was in essence different from the God of the New Testament. To him, Jesus was not virgin born nor was he the creator of the universe. The teachings of Marcion suggested an incoherence between the Jewish scriptures and the teachings of Christ and the apostles. 2 Tertullian wrote to combat this heresy and show "the connection between the Jewish and Christian Scriptures." 3

In book IV of his treatise against Marcion, Tertullian sets out to show that Christ was the creator, drawing most of his arguments from the gospel of Luke since it contained the only historical portion of the New Testament which Marcion accepted.4 In commenting on Luke 6:34-35, Tertullian taught that the eradication of usury as a first step would lead "more easily to accustom a man to the loss...of the money itself, the interest of which he had learnt to lose." He believed that the law (lending without interest) functioned as a preparation for the gospel (lending without expecting anything in return, including the principal) thus showing the consistency between the Old and New Testaments. 5

Constantine and the Triumph of the Church

As the Emperor Constantine's power grew more secure, "he favored Christianity more openly." By 317 "his coins dropped their pagan effigies", churches were exempted from taxation, needy congregations received money from the Emperor's treasury, new churches were built and the worship of images was forbidden. "The church rejoiced in blessings beyond any expectation... and all over the Empire Christians gathered in festal thanksgiving for the triumph of their God." 6

With political triumph came moral decline within the church. Shortly before A.D. 317, Cyprian complained "that his parishioners were mad about money" and bishops were becoming rich by lending money at usury. 7 During this period schism arose in the church regarding the Arian controversy. Arius claimed that Jesus Christ was a created being and that the Son did not exist eternally with his heavenly father. As the controversy spread Constantine "resolved to end it by calling the first ecumenical-universal-council of the Church." In 325 A.D. all bishops were summoned to Nicaea to answer this question and to settle disputes regarding other matters of the Church. 8

Canon XVII of the Council of Nicaea reads in part, "the holy and great Synod thinks it just that if after this decree any one (of the clergy) be found to receive usury, whether he accomplish it by secret transaction or otherwise, as by demanding the whole and one half, or by using any other contrivance whatever for filthy lucre's sake, he shall be deposed from the clergy and his name stricken from the list." [9] The canonist Van Espen commented on this Canon saying that "usury is forbidden by natural, by divine and by human law" and he noted that all the early councils ie...Elvira, Arles, Carthage, Tours, etc. condemned its practice. [10]

In an editorial comment, Henry Percival notes "there can be no doubt that Van Espen...has accurately represented and without any exaggeration the universal opinion of all teachers of morals, theologians, doctors, Popes, and Councils of the Christian Church for the first fifteen hundred years. All interest exacted upon loans of money was looked upon as usury, and its reception was esteemed a form of theft and dishonesty." [11]

Basil and Augustine

Basil (329-379) was bishop of the church at Caesarea and archbishop of Cappadocia and in all probability, the first Christian in history to found a hospital. Basil believed that God made some rich that they "may receive the reward of beneficence and faithful distribution." [12]

In a letter to Amphilochius, Basil answers several questions regarding the Church Canons and the interpretation of certain scriptures. Commenting on Canon XVII of the Council of Nicaea, Basil reinforces his ideas about the responsibility of the rich saying "a taker of usury, if he consent to spend his unjust gain on the poor, and to be rid of the future of the plague of covetousness, may be received into the ministry." [13] To Basil, a man who practiced usury eliminated himself from serving as God's minister in the church until he repented of this evil practice.

Augustine (354-430) is perhaps the best known of the later church fathers. [14] In one of his best known works, The City of God, Augustine attempts to "shore up the faith of his flock" during the siege of Rome by the Goths in 410 A.D. [15] Reflecting on the condition of Rome during the Punic Wars (ie...wars waged by Rome against Carthage 264 B.C.-146 B.C.) Augustine notes that the patricians (noblemen) began "to oppress the people as slaves, to condemn them to death or scourging, as the kings had done, to drive them from their holdings, and to tyrannize over those who had no property to lose." [16]

However, to Augustine these abusive tactics were not the worst occurrences of oppression, for the people were "overwhelmed... most of all by usury, and obliged to contribute both money and personal service to the constant wars." [17] Indeed, it is sobering to think that Augustine would classify the practice of usury on the same level as death, scourging, and the confiscation of property. As Christians we should seriously re-evaluate our beliefs about the morality of taking interest. The church fathers believed it to be the height of oppression.

Later Councils and the Middle Ages

Canon V of the African Code of 419 A.D. reads in part "the cupidity of avarice (which, let no one doubt, is the mother of all evil things), is to be henceforth prohibited, lest anyone should usurp another's limits, or for gain should pass beyond the limits fixed by the fathers, nor shall it be at all lawful for any of the clergy to receive usury of any kind... And what is reprehensible in laymen is worthy of still more severe censure in the clergy." A helpful note appended to Canon V states "as the taking of any kind of usury is condemned in laymen, much more is it condemned in clergymen." [18]

Canon X of the Quinisext Council of 692 A.D. stated that "a Bishop or presbyter, or deacon who receives usury... let him desist or be deposed." [19] The Lateran Council of 1139 and the third Lateran Council of 1179 both issued decrees denouncing the practice of usury. [20]

Thomas Aquinas, (1227-1274) following the Aristotilian tradition, condemned the "sin of usury." "To take usury for money lent is unjust in itself, because this is to sell what does not exist, and this evidently leads to inequality which is contrary to justice." [21]

To illustrate this truth, Aquinas used the example of wine and bread where the use of the item is transferred with the item itself. It would be unthinkable to loan someone a glass of wine or loaf of bread thinking they would not consume it. The transfer of goods of this nature is the transfer of ownership. "Accordingly if a man wanted to sell wine separately from the use of the wine, he would be selling the same thing twice, or he would be selling what does not exist, wherefore he would evidently commit a sin of injustice." [22]

To Aquinas, money was classified as this type of good whereby its proper and principal function was consumption. "Hence it is by its very nature unlawful to take payment for the use of money lent, which payment is known as usury: and just as a man is bound to restore other ill gotten goods, so is he bound to restore the money which he has taken in usury." [23]

The Protestant Reformation/Luther and Calvin

By the time of the Renaissance commerce and industry grew so rapidly that many believed that business could not dispense with interest. "They perceived that interest is the soul of credit, and that where credit is to exist to any considerable extent interest cannot be prohibited, and that suppressing interest means suppressing at least nine-tenths of all credit transactions." [24]

"The truth was that usury was practised by the whole of society: princes, the rich, merchants, the humble, and even the Church - by a society that tried to conceal the forbidden practice, frowned on it but resorted to it, disapproved of those who handled it, but tolerated them.... The Jews (because they were permitted to lend money to Gentiles) were as necessary as bakers." 25 During this period the Reformers emerged unshaken in the "theoretical conviction that loan interest was a parasitic gain... but consented to a practical compromise with the imperfection of man, on which it laid the blame for the obstinate vitality of loan interest." 26 Many feel that because of this compromise we have widespread usury today.

The reader should note that even though both Calvin and Luther accommodated to their age on the doctrine of usury, their writings frequently betrayed them. Bohm-Bawerk notes that in his earlier life Luther "had been a relentless enemy of usury." 27

In his classic biography on Luther, Roland Bainton observes that "Luther took his stand on the Deuteronomic prohibition of usury and the Aristotelian theory of the sterility of money. One gulden, said Luther, cannot produce another. The only way to make money is to work." 28

Commenting on Deuteronomy 23:19, Luther declared that "usury should not be demanded from a brother, but from a stranger." 29 To Luther, God permitted the Jews to exact usury from Gentiles because, as His chosen people, the Jews were "instruments of His wrath." 30 Apparently, Luther saw the taking of usury as an exercise of God's judgment on His enemies.

In a similar spirit the great reformer, John Calvin, blasted the practice of usury. In his commentary on Ezekiel 18:5-9, Calvin refers to it as a crime which "gnaws and by degrees consumes the miserable." He further equated the practice with "spoiling the wretched and sucking out their blood." [31] To illustrate the unworthiness of this "illiberal trade," Calvin showed how Cato saw usury "almost the same as murder" and that the "usurer will always be a robber."[32]

Calvin notes that societies in his day adopted new terminology to distinguish between interest and usury for the term "usury is odious." Regarding the French he notes that "since the name for interest was unknown to the French, that for usury became detestable: hence the French devised a new craftiness by which they could deceive God. For since no one could bear the name of usury, they used 'interest' instead."[33]

In England, David Hume, a proponent of usury, noted that "by a lucky accident in language, which has a great effect on men's ideas, the invidious word, usury, which formerly meant the taking of any interest for money, came now to express only the taking of exorbitant and illegal interest."[34] Similarly, the use of the word "usury" has all but been eliminated from our modern world. It seems like we too are trying to deceive God by a simple slight of the tongue. But "do not be deceived: God cannot be mocked. A man reaps what he sows" (Galatians 6:7).

Still Calvin believed that a rich man with a very good estate could borrow money from his neighbor at interest without his neighbor violating the law of God. Unfortunately Calvin does not quote scripture to justify his teaching on this point but instead leans upon human reasoning and understanding and the common practice of his day. However, Calvin concludes that "we must always hold that the tendency of usury is to oppress one's brother and hence it is to be wished that the very names of usury and interest were buried and blotted out from the memory of men."35

The Reformation entered the German state in 1546, the year of Luther's death. This region soon became a center of differing evangelical opinions. Frederick III "ordered a catechism to be written in an attempt to bring the people together. The men chosen for this important task were Zacharias Ursinus and Caspar Olevianus." The end result of their work was the Heidelberg Catechism named for the city in which it was written. 36

In answer to question #110 in the catechism, What doth God forbid in the eighth command? Ursinus replied "God forbids not only those thefts and robberies which are punishable by the magistrate, but he comprehends under the name of theft, all wicked tricks and devices, whereby we design to appropriate to ourselves the goods which belong to our neighbor; whether it be by force, or under the appearance of right, as by unjust weights, ells (a measure of length), measures, fraudulent merchandise, false coins, usury, or by any other way forbidden by God." 37 He defined usury as "the gain which is received in view of that which has been borrowed or loaned." Ursinus seemed perplexed by the many questions respecting usury and concluded that Christians should act according to the golden rule of Christ, "whatever ye would that men should do to you, do ye even so to them." 38

Regarding the Puritans of the 16th century, Leland Ryken notes that they were "overwhelmingly opposed to the practice of taking interest on money that had been lent. They were opposed to it because of Old Testament prohibitions against it and because of what they felt to be the spirit behind the practice, namely, covetousness and greed." It was not until society became more industrialized that Puritans made any distinction between usury and interest. 39

Later in the 17th century, Thomas Watson the Puritan, had this to say about an usurer. "He takes by extortion from others. He seems to help another by letting him have money in his necessity, but gets him into bonds, and sucks out his blood and marrow. I read of a woman whom Satan had bound and truly he is almost in as bad a condition whom the usurer has bound. The usurer is a robber." 40 Watson understood the true nature of usury as theft, extortion, murder and a tool to keep people in bondage.

Later Developments

According to Bohm-Bawerk, the greatest advances on the new doctrine of usury occurred in seventeenth century in the Netherlands. "There, transactions involving interest were common and regular; and there, moreover, temporal legislation had long since yielded to the pressure of practice and allowed the taking of interest." This change came about largely through the writings of Grotius, Salmasius and Massalia. 41

In Germany the change came more slowly. Toward the end of the seventeenth century theorists became "more generally convinced of the legitimacy of interest." The victory was hastened by the influence of Pufendorf and Leibnitz. 42

In England the "the rapid rise of its commerce and industry" rendered its economy favorable to the institution of interest. "Legislation had early given way to the needs of industrial life." By 1545 Henry VIII abolished laws prohibiting interest and installed a "simple legal rate." The prohibition was reinstated by Edward VI "but in 1571 it was once more repealed by Queen Elizabeth, and this time forever." England's most influential thinkers who promoted a more relaxed position on interest were Bacon, Locke and Bentham. 43 The thinking of these men has highly influenced monetary trends in America from colonial days to the present economic condition. Truly, "ideas-like actions-have consequences."

Contemporary Thought

In recent years Western Civilization has undergone a series of critical moral changes. The prohibition of gambling has been replaced by legal state lotteries. Abortion, once considered heinous, is now a mother's right. Pornography, which used to be considered trash, is hailed as a valiant expression of "freedom of speech." The uncommon practice of divorce now affects almost every household. Homosexuality and prostitution, words unfit to mention two or three decades ago, are now deemed alternative lifestyles.

The field of economics has likewise produced its moral changes. Sluggards can now gain wealth through government enforced wealth transfer programs and the sin of usury (interest) no longer exists. Policy makers concluded that with double digit inflation laws against usury (excessive interest) must be forgotten.

Financiers soon capitalized on the new liberation. A 62 year old, disabled woman in Washington D.C. found herself unemployed and unable to pay her bills. She obtained a one-year $25,000 mortgage with an "effective interst rate of 142 percent." A family in Flagstaff, Arizona, borrowed $700 at 127 percent interest while a couple in Virginia paid $2,100 to borrow $5,325. Other victims, "either gullible or desperate, lost their homes to the lenders."44

Today, interest rates are highly regulated in the United States by the Federal Reserve. If the Fed decides to raise interest rates the economy tends to slow down because fewer borrowers are willing to pay the higher costs of borrowing and investors are reluctant to provide funds that produce a low rate of return. Likewise, when the Fed wants to stimulate the economy they simply decide to lower the interest rate. Either way our entire monetary system is slavishly tied to credit spending and the use of usury. Current habits indicate no change for the future.

A Lesson From the Middle East

In the Arab world today usury remains immoral. Ironically, the Koran (the Moslem holy book) condemns the practice of charging interest. "That which you seek to increase by usury will not be blessed by Allah" (*The Koran,* The Greeks: 30:39). Among fundamentalist Moslems this prohibition survives as an important article of faith. According to William Greider, "Islamic societies...have never passed through the stages of capitalist development that changed the thinking of Western Christianity. The banking system that existed in the Middle East was largely superimposed by European colonialism, but its values were never accepted by the Moslem faithful."[45]

The Arab nations also provide an interesting alternative to Western banking. Their system serves as intermediary between depositors and borrowers. New capital is raised for perspective entrepreneurs without paying interest. "The investor would share equitably in the risk of the enterprise, profiting or losing as a partner with the entrepreneur...The investor is promised a fixed percentage of future profits, but he is not guaranteed that he will receive income or even the full return of his original principal."[46]

Conclusion

The early church carried on the traditions of the law and the teachings of Our Lord. The apostles freely gave to the benefit of all those who had need. Later, the church fathers condemned usury, equating it with murder, robbery and the vilest forms of oppression. The early church councils included canons stating the churches opposition to the taking of interest among clergy and laity alike. Not until the days of the reformation do we see a change among Christian apologists justifying the practice of usury. Undoubtedly even these reformers would cringe today if they could witness the financial practices among professing believers.

Christians must strive to keep out of debt and avoid the payment of usury. Strict discipline with our personal finances will encourage us to make cash purchases. When necessary, Christians should loan their surplus wealth to needy and destitute brothers without charging them interest. True children of the King will not even expect to receive back the principle amount loaned. Believers are free to loan their money at interest to those outside the family of faith. This practice should be used in hopes of leading such outsiders to personal faith in Christ.

Churches should remain debt free! The common practice of borrowing at interest by local assemblies of believers is unbiblical and should therefore be discouraged. Wealthy Christians (those without need) who insist on borrowing money to make money should be treated as foreigners and required to pay interest for the use of another's riches.

The writer does not suggest that Christians advocate the passing of legislation to make the practice of usury illegal. Such action would go beyond Biblical sanction. Obviously, the American people (Christians included) are no where close to stopping their infamous spending habits. We will continue to purchase goods with money we do not have at high interest rates until the system collapses or until we see light from God's word on the subject, confess our sin and repent. If the Christian community does not change its thinking in the matter of debt and interest, we cannot expect to see a change in the world. For those who are serious about getting out of financial bondage and remaining that way, may we suggest that you read on to the next chapter. May God bless you in your pursuit of debt free living!

Chapter Seven
The Marvel of Loan Pre-Payment

"Mortgage prepayment isn't a new idea, it's a renewed one. Its time has come again because a dollar of equity ownership is once again more valuable than a dollar of interest expense."

-John Cunningham-

Jake and Sue bought an average house in the suburbs for $94,000. They put $9,000 down and financed $85,000 at 10% for thirty years. This couple felt smug thinking how much money they would save over renting. Their monthly payments of $745 would be building them equity (they hoped).

Unfortunately they never learned what I discovered as a banker. Jake and Sue did not realize how long it would take before they accrued any noticeable equity on their home. At first they failed to comprehend "the real cost" of their new home if they followed the loan schedule to term. Payments, with interest, would total an unbelievable $277,560, or about three times the original purchase price.

If we had met Jake and Sue before they signed the papers, we may have discussed some of the disadvantages of premature home ownership (when a large mortgage is required). Unfortunately, young couples newly married no longer settle for a humble "fixer upper" as their first home. For many, renting is not even considered an option. They commonly seek to begin where there parents left off after decades of hard work. Most young marrieds want to have two cars and a large three or four bedroom home, fully furnished, when they move in. 1

Is buying always the best way to provide a home for your family? When we consider the cost of financing a home the actual net gain from equity can be minimal. Add to this the amount it costs for routine and unexpected maintenance, taxes and insurance and the profitability of owning a home can be drastically reduced. It does not always make best economic sense to buy your home.

Consider the following list of items which can cost a home-owner a bundle of money.

Roof	Plumbing
Lighting	Electrical Wiring
Heating System	Hot Water Tank
Appliances	Sewers
Doors & Windows	Air Conditioning
Gutters	Paint
Washer & Dryer	Dishwasher
Insect and pest control	Driveways & sidewalks
Carpeting	Fences
Trees & Shrubs	Floor Coverings
Insulation	Chimneys

Since we bought our house just six years ago we have had to replace the hot water tank ($300), paint the outside ($850), put on a new roof ($2,500), and buy two new screen doors ($300). In addition to this we suspect that we will be forced (by local government) to connect to the city sewer system. This has cost local Portland residents from 3 to 8 thousand dollars! One author notes how one family experienced the breakdown of their garbage disposal, dishwasher, and clothes washer at the same time. 2

This is not to say that buying a home is always the worst decision. Before deciding whether to rent or buy one must weigh all the factors and seek the Lord's guidance. As noted in the previous chapters on debt and usury the Bible does give specific teaching concerning your housing decision. The reader is encouraged to study the scriptures thoroughly before purchasing a home and becoming a servant to the lender for several years. (For a list of scripture references used in this book see Appendix A.)

We can conclude that providing a place for your family to live constitutes a need. However, this does not justify the purchase of a home beyond one's financial ability. Your down payment should be large enough so that your equity will be sufficient to cover any possible loss due to unforeseen foreclosure or forced sale of your property. In this way the house serves as your collateral on the loan.

Another precaution to take when borrowing for the purchase of a home is to insist that an "exculpatory" clause be contained in your loan contract. To exculpate means to exonerate or clear of a charge. According to Ron Blue, "an exculpatory clause literally means that the lender will exonerate you from having to repay the debt, taking back as full payment the asset that was used as collateral. There is, therefore, no personal liability...and it does allow you to repay without presuming upon the future." [3]

Housing needs do not necessarily have to be met by purchasing a home when adequate rentals are available. Before I got married I rented a two bedroom house for $300.00 a month. I never believed I was wasting money for the house provided shelter, comfort and storage for my possessions. Furthermore, I was relieved not to have the responsibility for the upkeep of the house. I was free to put my energies and money into other endeavors and I was living debt free.

The best possible solution for meeting your housing need lies in purchasing your home with cash, free and clear from all economic encumbrances. When borrowing money to buy a home one always runs the risk of losing his down payment investment along with the house. Good financial sense says "pay in cash and stay out of debt." Though some may not find themselves in such a position, it would be good to instruct and encourage our children to practice the debt free lifestyle now so that when they mature they can purchase their home without the assistance of the local money lender.

Since Jake and Sue already borrowed money to purchase their home we want to focus on sharing the secret of loan prepayment. The remainder of this chapter centers on those who, like Jake and Sue, have already purchased a home with a long term loan at interest. In practical terms this is perhaps the most important chapter of this book. Wise stewards of earthly wealth will take personal responsibility for their future economic stability by getting out of debt now! While some may want to consider buying down by selling a more expensive home for a cheaper one, this section is devoted to showing you how to save time and money by prepaying your mortgage. The principles discussed apply to any type of loan.

What is Pre-Payment?

Marc Eisenson defines pre-payment as "a payment in advance of its due date... the term implies small advance payments applied toward the outstanding balance, at either Regular or Irregular intervals, during the loan's term". 4 For instance if Jake and Sue would increase their mortgage payment by only $26 a month, they could cut five years off of their payments. With a total additional sum of only $1,560 they would save $36,815 in interest!

According to their original contract, Jake and Sue would pay interest charges totalling $183,565, enough to purchase two more homes of equal value. Simply by increasing their monthly payments by $74 a month they would decrease their loan by ten years and save an astonishing $71,666. An increase of $167 a month would cut the loan's term in half and save an incredible $104,116, almost $20,000 more than the original basis of the loan. That's incredible!

Many people erroneously believe that the borrower must stick to his original payment plan and that any advance pre-payments are not allowed. According to John Cunningham there are only four requirements when you take out a loan. First, you must pay back the entire loan amount. Second, you can take no longer than the agreed term of your loan. Third, you can pay no less than the normal monthly payment. Finally, interest is paid only on the outstanding balance. [5]

Methods of Pre-Payment

Constant Payment Plan

Perhaps the simplest type of pre-payment is the Constant Payment Plan. This involves regular monthly pre-payments of a determined amount, usually in $25.00 increments. The following schedules will give you some idea of how much can be saved simply by adding a few extra dollars to your mortgage payment each month.

Table 1

$50,000.00 for 30 Years @ 12% Interest

Pre-Pmt Amt	Dollars Saved	Mthly Pmts Saved
$ 25.00	$43,199.00	96
50.00	61,965.00	141
100.00	81,322.00	190
200.00	98,714.00	238

Table 2

$85,000 for 30 Years @ 9% Interest

Pre-Pmt	AmtDollars Saved	Mthly Pmts Saved
$ 25.00	$28,464.00	52
50.00	46,858.00	88
100.00	70,188.00	135
200.00	95,110.00	189

The reader should keep in mind that the greatest savings from pre-payment occur at the front or beginning of your loan when the interest portion of your payment is higher. Consequently the constant payment plan will save you less toward the end of your obligation. None the less, this type of pre-payment plan is simple and will save you money and time. Instead of giving all those interest dollars to the bank why not put them to work for yourself.

To assist you in this type of program ask your bank to prepare you a repayment schedule which includes your pre-payment amount. This will help you see the effects and final results of your extra efforts. Also it will insure that your bank is applying your extra payments properly.

The Shifting Payment Plan

This payment plan is named for its inconsistent pre-payment amount. People who utilize this method take whatever is left over from their monthly expenses and apply it to their mortgage payment. It functions much like the constant payment plan above but with some distinct disadvantages.

First, this method is unpredictable. You never know how much will be applied to your debt in any given month making goal setting very difficult to achieve. In addition this method allows you to easily miss a pre-payment because there will always be that unexpected expense during the month.

Periodic One-Time Payments

When a person receives a large amount of extra income he will sometimes apply the funds as a one-time pre-payment to his loan. Some examples might include a federal or state tax return, proceeds from the sale of property or negotiable securities, funds earned from maturing bonds or an inheritance from someone's estate. According to John Cunningham this lump-sum method is the "choice for people such as farmers and owners of vacation businesses who receive their incomes seasonally." [6]

The difficulty in this method rests in the unlikelihood of most people receiving such extra cash flow. Consequently the majority of borrowers will not be consistent in making pre-payments using this plan. Also, when we receive a little extra cash we usually think of a million other things we need to buy with the money and the mortgage gets neglected. This method works ideally in conjunction with a more consistent plan. Determine ahead that you will make pre-payments each month and any additional money applied from one-time lump sums can be considered bonus payments.

Paying Next Months Principal in Advance

This type of pre-payment allows you to make your regular monthly payment with the next outstanding principal amount added to the sum remitted. To use this method it will be necessary for the borrower to obtain a repayment schedule (amortization schedule) from your lending institute.

If your bank or savings and loan cannot provide this report for you there are computer software programs available that have such capability or write to the author at Back Home Industries (see end notes at the back of the book for information).[7] Be sure that your repayment schedule begins with your current balance.

Keep in mind that this plan saves you more interest expense at the beginning of your loan and most people abandon this method once 50% of the original amount has been paid. The following schedules will help you visualize how this plan works.

Table 3

Calculating Current Month Interest

Balance	$85,000.00
Interest Rate	x12%
Yearly Interest	$ 7,650.00
Months (Divide)	12
Current Month's Interest	$ 637.50

Table 4

Amortization Schedule $85,000.00 for 30 Years @ 9% Interest
$683.93 Per Month: First Year

Pmt #	Interest	Principal	Balance
1	$637.50	$46.43	$84,953.57
2	637.15	46.78	84,906.79
3	636.80	47.13	84,859.66
4	636.45	47.48	84,812.18
5	636.09	47.84	84,764.34
6	635.73	48.20	84,716.14
7	635.37	48.56	84,667.58
8	635.01	48.92	84,618.66
9	634.64	49.29	84,569.37
10	634.27	49.66	84,519.71
11	633.90	50.03	84,469.68
12	633.52	50.41	84,419.27

When the first payment comes due, the debtor must pay $683.93 of which only $46.43 is applied to the principal. If he pays an additional $46.78 (principal payment #2) or a total of $730.71 he will save the interest charges from the second payment or $637.15. When the next payment is remitted the borrower will pay a total of $731.41 ($683.93 + 47.48) because he is actually paying the principal for the next two payments (ie...payments 3 & 4) while paying the interest only on the current payment due (ie... payment #3 or $636.80). This will save him an additional $636.45 or the interest he would have normally paid for payment number four. Any principal paid in advance saves you that months interest charges!

After six months of regular next month principal pre-payments the borrower has reduced his obligation by one year. The following schedule shows his monetary savings for this six month period.

Table 5

Schedule of Interest Savings

Pmts Pre-Paid	Principal Pre-Paid	Int Saved
# 2	$46.78	$637.15
# 4	47.48	636.45
# 6	48.20	635.73
# 8	48.92	635.01
#10	49.66	634.27
#12	50.41	633.52
Totals	$291.45	$3,812.13

By pre-paying $291.45 on the first six payments one saves an incredible $3,812.13 in interest charges. Some may counter saying that they cannot afford to make the extra payments each month. However, we must remember if we do not pre-pay principal now we will pay all the interest later, whether we like it or not! One must decide who gets your hard earned money. Pre-pay a little now and invest in yourself or pre-pay nothing now and pay the bank. Simply stated, pre-payment makes economic sense and is perhaps the best way to save money.

Bi-Weekly Scheduled Payments

Many financial institutes have adopted bi-weekly mortgage plans where your payments are split into two equal portions and paid every two weeks. Because there are 26 bi-weeks in a year you actually make two extra annual payments equivalent to one additional monthly payment. Normally, bi-weekly payment schedules must be initiated from the inception of your loan.

Using the following example we can discover the financial advantage of the biweekly plan. It takes $683.93 each month for 30 years to retire an $85,000 loan at 9% interest. The total finance charges on such a loan amounts to $161,214.80. Set up with biweekly payments of $341.97 this loan would be paid in 21 years and 48 weeks, a reduction of 8 years and 4 weeks. The savings on the interest paid to you instead of the bank would amount to $51,359.89.

Conclusion

In light of current economic trends Christians must take immediate action to get out of debt and remain financially free. Across the country, real estate value has decreased making investments in property less desirable and economically unstable. Many experts believe that another "great depression" is inevitable.

Mortgage pre-payment makes sense and can save us literally thousands of hard earned dollars. One should find the pre-payment plan which best fits his needs and then put that plan into undelayed action. The several methods discussed in this chapter included the constant payment plan, the shifting payment plan, periodic one time payment plan, paying next months principal plan and the biweekly payment plan. Customized plans can also be developed to coincide more closely with specific individual loans. Some may simply need to sell their home and re-establish their financial goals or purchase a home of lesser value.

In spite of all the evidence showing the value of pre-payment some still remain unconvinced and insist that they cannot afford to make extra principal payments each month. Actually you cannot afford not to pre-pay your loan. To assist the doubting Thomases we will give some money saving tips in the next chapter which should help you in adding funds to your disposable income to pre-pay your mortgage.

Still others maintain that they need to pay the

interest in order to receive the tax deduction. These people fail to realize that they continue to get the tax benefit while making their regular monthly payments. Pre-payments are simply additions to these regular payments. According to John Cunningham "your actual tax deduction doesn't really begin to fall until the last five years of the mortgage." [8]

Furthermore, interest expense is treated as a "reduction in the amount of income that is subject to taxation" and is not a tax credit where you get a dollar for dollar reduction in your taxes. [9] For instance "if you are in the 28 percent tax bracket you would normally be taxed 28 cents for each $1.00 of income. However, for each $1.00 that is spent on interest expense your tax bill is reduced by 28 cents." [10] Obviously you would be spending $1.00 in interest to save 28 cents in taxes. One can easily see that in such a transaction you lose 72 cents on every dollar.

In the next chapter we will not only give some money saving tips but also some helpful suggestions for you to consider in making safe investments in a troubled economy. May we as stewards of God's kingdom learn to make the most of our financial resources in such way as to bring glory and honor to His Name.

Chapter Eight
The Value of Thrift

"Men do not realize how great an income thrift is."

-Cicero-

John D. Rockefeller seemed a very unlikely candidate to become a multi-millionaire. His father struggled as a peddler and barely made ends meet. However, he taught John how to earn money and keep it. John's mother instructed him to put God first in his life, while practicing honesty and charity with his neighbors. Rockefeller declared; "From the beginning I was trained to work, to save, and to give." [1]

John went on to establish the Standard Oil Company. In business he continually sought ways to save money. "He built his refineries well and bought no insurance. He also employed his own plumber and almost halved the cost of labor, pipes, and plumbing materials." Rockefeller continually reinvested his profits into his business providing bigger and better equipment and a broader range of products at cheaper costs to consumers. [2]

In the course of his life Rockefeller was faithful with his tithe. "From the time of his first job, where he earned 50 cents a day, the 16 year old Rockefeller gave to his local Baptist church, to missions in New York City and abroad, and to the poor - black or white. As his salary increased, so did his giving. By the time he was 45 he was up to $100,000 per year; at age 53, he topped the $1,000,000 mark in his annual giving. His eightieth year was his most generous: $138,000,000 he happily gave away." 3

Thrift and Increase

Richard Cobden once noted that, "the world has always been divided into two classes: those who have saved, and those who have spent; the thrifty and the extravagant. The building of all the houses, the mills, the bridges, and the ships, and the accomplishment of all other great works which have rendered man civilized and happy, has been done by the savers - the thrifty; and those who have wasted their resources have always been their slaves." 4

Thrift, economy and saving produce tomorrow's wealth. Without such virtues society will be reduced to poverty. Samuel Budgett claimed that the lack of these doomed hundreds of business men to failure. "Economy was one of the cardinal lessons he taught his six hundred clerks." 5

While walking with one of his servant girls down an old country highway, Mr. Budgett found a potato. He graciously handed it to the girl and proceeded to give her a lecture on economy. Budgett promised her the use of some land to plant the potato and its increased crop each year. The young lady accepted the pledge and immediately planted her potato.

"The yield was thirteen potatoes the first year, ninety-three the second year, and a barrel full the third year, and had the experiment been continued for fifty years Budgett could not have found land enough in England on which to plant the last crop." 6 Had the young girl eaten the potato upon receiving it from Mr. Budgett she would not have reaped any future reward. The lesson she learned illustrates the practical advantage of economy and the law of increase that follows. 7

Making Your Money Work for You

We live in a generation where saving money for future needs is considered anathema. On one side stand the pietists who say that having any kind of savings account shows a lack of faith in God to supply for your every need. They advocate giving away any extra funds not needed for your immediate expenses. On the other side the Keynesians (pronounced like "cane") champion the cause of spending our way to prosperity. 8

The economic doctrine of this second school of thought has dominated higher education and monetary policy in the United States since 1936, when John Maynard Keynes' book, *The General Theory*, was first published. Keynes taught that consumption, extravagance and improvidence were great virtues to embrace while saving, thrift and financial prudence constituted detestable vices to be avoided. 9

The result of implementing his theory reveals a dramatic decline in United States savings since 1944. In that year Americans saved 36.9 billion dollars or 25.2% of their disposable income. By 1947 this figure dropped to 4 billion dollars or 2.4% of disposable income. After a few years of minor recoveries, not to exceed 19.8 billion dollars or 7.9% of disposable income, the total savings fell again in 1955 to 17.1 billion dollars or 6.3% of disposable income. [10] Estimates today disclose American savings at only 2% of disposable income, "the lowest saving rate in the industrial world... and also the lowest saving rate in our own history." [11]

Saving has been defined as "the process of refraining from consuming a part of production." [12] Thus, savings is a surplus of cash reserved for future consumption or production. As we discussed earlier, this generation thrives on instant gratification and lacks patience and self control in their purchasing habits. In order to set aside money for the future or pay off current debt we must first learn to defer our indulgent inclinations which consumer goods and deficit spending provide.

The following suggestions are intended to assist you in accumulating extra cash for getting you out of debt sooner and on your way to establishing a regular savings plan.

Enhance Income

A normal inclination to generate extra cash to pay off financial obligations is for husbands to take on additional employment or for wives to leave the home and family to secure a regular paying job. Although these are options, we do not recommend them.

A vital factor in family restoration lies in the

biblical injunction for women to love their husbands and children and for them to be workers at home (Titus 2:4-5). With mom working outside the home, it becomes difficult or impossible to home school your children and often times the working woman finds herself surrounded by many temptations which cause her to question her love for her husband.

Similarly, the man who spends all of his time away from the home, working two jobs can lose control of his family and his influence as head of the household begins to wane. Likewise he becomes susceptible to the allurement of the wayward woman whose flattering tongue seduces him and whose grasp reduces him to a crust of bread (Proverbs 6:24-29). How happy is the man who rejoices in the wife of his youth, finds satisfaction with her breasts at all times and is enraptured with her love (Proverbs 5:15-20). Husbands must cherish and care for their wives and keep them from becoming another man's slave.

These biblical mandates should not be taken to mean that a woman is limited to changing diapers, washing dishes and preparing meals. Women can be very creative in bringing in additional income for the family simply by using their homes as a place of business or for what some call a "cottage industry." By using their skills and homes efficiently, wives can be a good source of needed income to help retire debts early.

Home Business Ventures

The following list from Proverbs 31 illustrates

the number of opportunities available to the woman who desires to start a "cottage industry" in her own home. Notice the industriousness and creativity of this virtuous woman.

1. She willingly works with her hands making garments from the wool and flax she sought and purchased in the market. This woman reveled in the work of making suitable garments for her family and neighbors to enjoy. Although she extends her hand to the poor and the needy she also sells some of her wares for profit. Many wives have the dexterity and knowledge to indulge in this type of business venture. Even if you choose not to make clothes for resale, the money saved by making clothes for your own family will reduce your own household expenses considerably.

2. She seeks the best foods and sometimes gets up while it is still dark to prepare them for her family. Some women possess a real talent for cooking, baking and food preparation. Diligence in the kitchen can provide extra income from the sale of such items as bread, pies, and cakes. Those who have such talent should seek the many ways of using their ability to produce added income for the family. Mothers can also bring their children into this money making adventure.

3. From her profits she buys a field and plants a vineyard. This woman does not waste her hard earned money, but immediately puts it to work by acquiring land on which to make additional income. A

housewife who owns a little plot of land can turn that piece of land into household revenue by planting fruits and vegetables for the community to purchase.

4. She perceives that her merchandise is good. Undoubtedly this energetic woman traded with the merchants from her storehouse of products and she was well oriented with the market to make a profit for her family.

In his classic commentary on the book of Proverbs, Charles Bridges says this about the industrious homemaker. "Her several employments admirably illustrate genuine simplicity of manners, and practical, yet liberal economy. This is indeed a difficult and rare attainment, economy without a niggardly (stingy) spirit; seen and felt as little as possible, and conducted with all care and consideration of the comfort of the family." [13]

Husbands must remember not to over work their wives in a desire to get out of debt. Likewise we cannot expect them to contribute all the money making endeavors mentioned in Proverbs 31. These are to be looked at as opportunities for possible income producing side ventures rather than mandatory norms for a spiritual helpmeet. Also if our wives are taking time out of their busy schedules to bring in additional income then we may need to help with the teaching and training of the children and the management of the home.

Although added income from a home industry can boost a family's household budget, a wife's job outside of the home often contributes little or no actual net gain. It is not uncommon for the wife's income to be lost in extra clothes expenses, increased outside meals, more convenience foods for the home, higher taxes, baby-sitter's fees, travel costs, additional expenses created by the job, and I-deserve-it-rewards to compensate for all the extra work.

George Fooshee describes this delusion. "One of my friends is a business executive. His wife works part time...When he figured his taxes this year, he noted that 58% of all she earned went out for federal, state, and Social Security taxes. When I asked him if she spent only 42% of what she made, he just laughed."[14]

Mary LaGrand Bouma in The Creative Homemaker explains how a committed homemaker can often make more of a financial contribution to the family than a woman working outside of the home. She tells the story of a young mother with two preschool children who felt compelled to work until they could get out of debt.

> They could not manage to keep a babysitter for the children so they were shifted from one temporary place to another. Their father worried that they were losing contact with the children. Finally, the mother was forced to quit her job, as she was expecting twins. Seven months later she sheepishly admitted to my husband that because she stayed home the family had gotten out of debt! She explained that she had started to do her own baking, and she began to fix economical meals. She enjoyed cooking, and keeping the cost low became a challenge to her. She also stopped buying so many of the expensive cosmetics she had not been able to resist when she saw them every day. There were many other savings which she was able to make, all of which added up to more than her previous earnings. [15]

Pay Raises

Another source of additional income arises from periodic salary increases. Normally, instead of saving this extra cash or applying it to outstanding debts we raise our standard of living and consume all the increase. The diligent wage earner will resist this temptation and apply his pay raises to decrease his current debt, and become financially free as soon as possible.

Sell Unnecessary Possessions

The sale of household assets can be a good source of income to apply to your outstanding debts. My wife and I have operated a couple of our own garage sales which produced a small income for the family. Remember, even a small pre-payment on your mortgage of $50 or $100 can save you hundreds of dollars in interest. You not only save money by selling some of your possessions but you rid your home of unnecessary clutter. The sale of larger assets, such as a car or boat, if applied to your loan, could literally save you thousands of dollars of interest.

Reduce Expenses

Ron Blue notes that in "almost every family budget, as much as 30 to 40 percent could be used to repay debt." [16] The following suggestions are provided to assist the reader with expense reducing ideas.

Saving for the Big Expenses

All of us incur obligations which may need to be budgeted on a bimonthly or quarterly basis. Automobile insurance and life insurance normally fall under this category. Since these are known expenses funds can be set aside in advance each month for immediate payment when the bills come due. Under no circumstances should we allow ourselves to borrow money at high interest rates to pay for such items.
This same principle applies to home owners in paying their property taxes. If your taxes are not paid with your monthly mortgage, funds must be set aside each month, preferably in a savings account, so that when it comes time to pay your duties you already have the needed cash. These simple, common sense ideas can save you hundreds of dollars in interest expense and keep you out of financial bondage.
Similarly, money saved for unexpected repairs on appliances and automobiles can keep you from borrowing money and paying the bank unnecessary interest. Saving money for future necessities is not a sin, but rather a wise use of earthly riches. On the other hand, storing up riches simply to hoard it and spend it on your selfish desires is sinful and not what we are suggesting.

Transact Business with Cash

Operating on a strictly cash basis can save you

money and deliver you from the temptation of over spending. Studies have shown how those who use credit cards instinctively spend about 35% more than those who pay cash. Using cash instead of credit cards makes good sense and allows you to set aside extra dollars toward pre-paying your mortgage or saving for future expenses.

"Last year," reports Howard Dayton, Jr.,"it was necessary for Bev and me to get a second vehicle. We listed our requirements: a small pickup truck, in good mechanical condition, at a price of less than $500. We then prayed.

After three months a neighbor learned of our search. He owned a low mileage Datsun pickup in reasonable condition. He needed the truck once a month, but could no longer afford the insurance.

We bought the truck with the understanding that he could drive it the one day a month it was needed. The cost--$100!...By purchasing the low-cost used truck, we have been able to save the amount that would have been going toward car payments. Each month we put the "car payment" in a separate savings account to accumulate enough cash to pay for our next car...The key you can use to break the car financing habit is to begin saving now for your next car." [17]

<u>Control or Destroy Your Credit Cards</u>

In the United States today there are more than 700 million credit cards in circulation for a population of 240 million people. This means that six credit cards exist for each American adult. Businesses and credit card companies charge an average of 18.86% interest on the use of their cards and stand to lose about 5% of the outstanding balances. The millions of customers who routinely and faithfully pay their bills actually make up for the losses of the negligent. [18]

As we discussed earlier if one uses a credit card wisely by not incurring interest on his charges, he is not presuming on the future. However, we want to stress the importance of paying your credit card charges in full each month as the bill comes due. Before making any purchases with your card be sure you have enough money to cover the expenditure. When you get home write a check for the amount and hold it until you receive the bill. If this is not practical then be sure to include the amount when you pay your bills at the first of the month.

Lack of control in the use of your cards can easily lead to financial bondage. If you cannot completely pay your bill each month you should destroy your card. Reports show that one out of six people who use credit incur financial problems. [19] The quickest way into trouble is by misusing credit cards. We do not want to see Christians become another debt statistic.

Do Your Own Repair Work

A major cause of unexpected expense occurs when the machines and products of our modern technology break down. We need to prepare ahead of time for such failures. The most common items susceptible to malfunction and repair include cars, appliances,

home heating systems, plumbing and electricity.
When these things need maintenance it would be a good idea for us to consider taking the responsibility of fixing them ourselves. Labor costs run extremely high and each time we fix something on our own we save money. I would not consider myself a handyman around the house. As a matter of fact I hate doing repair work, but I have done minor repairs on all the items mentioned above in order to cut expenses.
Doing your own maintenance will mean an original outlay of cash to buy some tools, and repair manuals. The money you will save more than compensates for the expenditure. A few years ago I invested in some good automotive tools so I could do some of my own repair work on our cars. I have never been sorry for making this investment, and with two cars it was almost mandatory that some of the routine maintenance be done myself. To avoid going into debt to cover these unexpected repairs you will need to set aside a certain portion of your income each pay period.

Second Hand Stores

Some may not like the idea of shopping at thrift stores but our experience tells us that lots of money can be saved by utilizing such outlets. Just today my wife bought a needed blanket in "like new" condition at the local St.Vincent de Paul store for about five dollars.
Items such as clothing, bedroom furnishings, lamps, furniture, kitchen accessories, appliances and

tools can all be purchased at great savings from second hand stores. In the past I have purchased men's suits in excellent condition for less than twenty dollars. Wives will enjoy the dollars saved on the purchase of clothing for their rapidly growing children. These savings can be plowed right into your mortgage debt to help you become financially free years ahead of schedule.

Budget Meals

Wives who spend time preparing meals wisely and shopping carefully for food can save a family added dollars. My wife Wanda, a conscientious homemaker, states that "grocery shopping is a major area where pre-planning saves money. Shopping lists from pre-planned menus prevent waste in groceries." Women who work at home have the advantage of thoughtfully preparing their menus and shopping for bargains. [20]

Wanda reminds us that "only a portion of each earned dollar reaches the worker. Money is deducted from paychecks for taxes, retirement, and so forth"... but "when a woman saves a dollar from grocery spending, she saves a complete dollar"... and is "able to contribute as much or more to the family income as a woman working full time outside the home." [21]

We may also need to cut back on restaurant dining in order to reduce our food budget. Remember, all savings can be turned into debt reduction and will spare you hundreds or even thousands of dollars in interest expense.

Save Your Loose Change

Whenever you receive change from cash transactions, instead of spending the money, try putting the coins in a jar. Then periodically take the money to the bank and deposit it to your account for application to your home mortgage. I have heard where families actually saved more than $500 in one year simply by using this simple method.

Conclusion

The true measure of whether or not we really know God and love the Lord Jesus Christ is by keeping His commandments (1 John 2:1-4 & John 14:15 & 21). When God uses us to make new disciples of all nations we are to teach them to observe all things that Jesus Christ commanded (Matthew 28:20).

Because Christians have failed to fully instruct new converts, "we have seen 'conversions' that made no difference in how people lived." [22] In order to witness changed lives in Christian converts and keep people out of poverty, believers must begin to teach the whole counsel of God. This includes teaching people the "Biblical principles and practices of justice, economics, personal financial management, work, saving, staying out of debt, and caring for one's family." [23]

The next section will give you some helpful ideas on how you can invest your money and become more prosperous.

Chapter Nine
Investing for the Future

"By doing good with his money, a man, as it were, stamps the image of God upon it, and makes it pass current for the merchandise of heaven."

-John Rutledge-

The attorney looked worried as he reviewed the document. "You surely do not appreciate the meaning of this word. It is not my business, even though I am your attorney, to dissuade you and your wife from giving your personal wealth for the promotion of Christian work, if that is your wish; but I consider it my duty to point out the serious implications of this word 'irrevocable'. If you allow it to stand, it means that..."

"That I can't take it back again, even if I want to," retorted Mr. LeTourneau. "That if an emergency arises, and I am short of money, I cannot dip my hand into this fund. That my children will have no claim upon it. I know all that, but all the same, that word 'irrevocable' has to stand. Do you think that my wife and I want to give this to the Lord today, and take it back again tomorrow?" The lawyer was accustomed to witnessing the LeTourneaus give away large sums of money but "this latest idea of theirs, involving the signing away of ninety-eight per cent of their means, bewildered him." 1

The story of R.G. LeTourneau graphically illustrates how a small business beginning at home can grow beyond a person's wildest imagination. Faced with a $5,000.00 debt as a result of his partner's irresponsibility, Robert LeTourneau took on a job as a tractor repair man at a local ranch. Here Robert and his wife Evelyn paid off their debt and managed to save a little extra for the future. Six months later an incident occurred which changed the lives of this industrious couple. 2

The owner of the ranch asked Robert to level a piece of land. Robert agreed, thinking that making machines operate would be more fun than just repairing them. However, the equipment was a "ramshackle combination" which took two men to operate. If the operators fell out of synchronization (which happened frequently) the machine could be damaged and tempers would fly. By converting the machine from compressed air power to electrical power, Robert was able to control both the tractor and the blade used to change the contour of the land. This simple invention lead him to conclude that the land levelling business had possibilities. He later concentrated his efforts on the design and production of heavy, earth moving equipment. 3

Under the skies of California, Robert and Evelyn started their first small business utilizing a field at the side of their house. This venture grew "until it took its place among the large industrial concerns of the United States." 4 "In 1930...sales totalled nearly

$111,000, with a net profit of $34,474....In 1934 the advance was phenomenal, sales falling little short of a million dollars, with profits exceeding $340,000." 5

"For the year 1935 sales totalled two million dollars, and profits well over half-a-million; in 1936 sales passed the four million figure, and profits rose to $1,364,393; next year and the next showed a continued upward trend, until, by 1940, the sales of this company had exceeded ten million dollars, with a profit approaching two millions. But that was not the peak, for a year later sales figures had been nearly doubled; and by 1944, R.G. LeTourneau Incorporated recorded total takings of over forty two million dollars." 6

Although R.G. LeTourneau made and spent millions he likewise gave a large portion of his income for Christian endeavors. He saw money "as a means to produce the machine his mind has conceived or as a means to bring men to God." 7 He often said: **"The question is not how much of my money I give to God, but rather how much of God's money I keep for myself."** 8

In 1935 the LeTourneaus created their special foundation "described as a not-for-profit corporation whose income and capital can be used only for the Cause of Christ." In May 1947, it was valued at seven million dollars. 9 The remarkable life of R.G. LeTourneau reveals how the wise investment of earthly wealth can be used for making additional income and advancing the kingdom of God.

Investment Ideas

In this final section we want to provide the reader with some information which should prove helpful in your quest to invest your hard earned money most profitably. We do not claim to be financial advisors and leave your final decisions up to you and any experts in whom you choose to confide. Also, many books have been written on the subject and we recommend that you consult some before you make any investment decisions. We supply the following information as a brief introduction to the investment world.

<u>Self Employment and Home Industries</u>

According to a poll taken by Yankelovich, Skelly and White "nearly one-third of American workers would prefer to earn their livelihood at home"...and the Wall Street Journal "reports that an estimated 11 million people are already working from home." [10]

The benefits of working from your own home or being self employed are numerous. You gain a certain liberty which you do not possess when working for someone else. Usually you can make your own work schedule and take advantage of day light hours when needed. There is a certain amount of increased happiness doing what you want to do instead of working just to make a living. Being your own boss carries added responsibility but usually this is off-set with the satisfaction of knowing that you are calling the shots.

Other benefits from self employment and working from the home include, saving money from commuting expenses and baby sitting, closer involvement with your family and neighborhood and cutting costs by working and living from the same location. Some feel that working for yourself from the home causes less stress.

Self employment does not normally mean less work. Usually the opposite is true and working up to twice as many hours as a salaried job is not uncommon. Profits from your new business may take from two to five years to materialize so new entrepreneurs need to plan ahead and set aside ample funds to survive in case income is delayed. Planning is essential in any money making endeavor. If you "fail to plan" then "plan to fail."

In her book, Homemade Money, Barbara Brabec notes that 27% of all small businesses (home businesses included) fail in 3 years or less, 55% in 5 years or less and 82% in 10 years or less. Statistics indicate that 95% of these failures are caused by poor management. [11] A person going into his or her own business needs to remember that the determination to borrow money to finance the operation is a management decision. One of the greatest causes for business failure which falls into the poor management category is business debt.

We suggest that people who decide to engage in a family industry at home begin with the resources already available. Then as the Lord blesses add to your business investment the needed equipment or tools by paying for them with cash. Avoiding debt to finance your business venture insures a better chance of survival.

The following list provides the reader with some possible ideas for his or her own self employment opportunities.

<u>Automobile</u>
  Tune-ups
  Brake Repair
  Body work
  Mechanical
  Electrical
  Transmissions

<u>Business</u>
  Accountant
  Bookkeeper
  Child Day Care
  Income Tax Returns
  Salesman
  Real Estate Agent
  Appraiser
  Lawn and Garden Care
  Chimney Sweep
  Photographer
  Appliance Repair
  Bicycle Repair
  Secretarial/Typist
  Carpenter
  Plumber
  Painter
  Electrician

<u>Arts and Crafts</u>
  Writer
  Public Speaker
  Class Instructor
  Tutor
  Ceramics
  Furniture
  Interior Decorator
  Doll Making
  Jewelry
  Leatherworks
  Housewares
  Blankets
  Clothing
  Curtains
  Stuffed Animals
  Baking
  Canning
  Musician
  Music Instructor
  Printing
  Calligraphy
  Antiques
  Stained Glass
  Cartoonist
  Oil Painting

U.S. Government Securities

One of the safest investments you can make is in securities backed by the Treasury of the United States. Most investors believe that in a time of crises the U.S. Government will be the last institution to default. If it collapses every other investment is likely to crumble with the exception of gold and other precious metals.

Besides the safety feature, investors enjoy the advantage of liquidity that government securities provide. This means that these instruments can easily be turned into cash because there's normally another lender ready to buy your loan. Government securities are loans made to the government which it promises to repay by a specified date at a promised interest rate. The most common types of government securities are:

Treasury Bills which represent borrowing that the Treasury will repay in one year or less.

Treasury Notes which represent borrowing that the Treasury will repay in a 2 to 10 year period.

Treasury Bonds which represent long term government borrowing lasting from 10 years to as long as 30 years.

Savings Bonds are small loans made to the government by those who perhaps do not have the money for higher priced investments. These can be purchased through payroll savings plans.

Treasury securities can be purchased through banks, brokers and directly from the Treasury or the Regional Federal Reserve banks and branches. Government investments can also be made through Money Market Funds and personal IRA accounts. [12]

Precious Metals

We are living in inflationary times. Because of the increase of the money supply (ie...political Federal Reserve Notes or paper currency) the value of the dollar has decreased. In our own country during the fight for independence, the colonies were flooded with Continental notes to finance the war. As the paper money supply increased, its value in the market decreased. Soon the currency became difficult to exchange for goods and in 1779 George Washington declared "a wagon load of money will scarcely purchase a wagon load of provisions." [13]

This situation remained the same until 1781 when the value of the Continental dropped so low that it ceased from circulating in the colonies. Clarence Carson notes that "gold and silver coins came out of hiding and replaced paper money as the currency of the land." [14]

A similar scenario appeared in France during the years of 1789-1796. Paper money circulated widely and the purchasing power of the French franc plummeted dramatically. Andrew Dickson White visualizes the enormous decline by providing the following chart in American equivalents: 15

	1790	1795
A bushel of flour	$.40	45.00
A bushel of oats	.18	10.00
A cartload of wood	4.00	500.00
A bushel of coal	.07	2.00
A pound of sugar	.18	12.50
A pound of soap	.18	8.00
A pound of candles	.18	8.00
A head of cabbage	.08	5.50
A pair of shoes	1.00	40.00
Twenty five eggs	.24	5.00

White goes on to describe the end of the crises; "when all was over with paper money, specie (coined money ie...gold and silver) began to reappear-first in sufficient sums to do the small amount of business which remained after the collapse. Then as the business demand increased, the amount of specie flowed in from the world at large to meet it, and the nation gradually recovered from that long paper-money debauch.... But though there soon came a degree of prosperity... convalescence was slow.... It required fully forty years to bring capital, industry, commerce and credit up to their condition when the Revolution began." 16

Like those mentioned above, "all great inflations end with the acceptance of real money-gold-and the rejection of political money-paper." 17 Historically, when governments take it upon themselves to create money they always over extend themselves and plunge their citizens into precarious predicaments. It is the individuals concern and responsibility in an inflationary age to take the necessary action to protect himself and his family from such irresponsible government.

One consideration toward meeting this goal is the purchase of precious metals. Even if the economy collapses and paper money loses its value, gold and silver will maintain its purchasing power. Gold and other precious metals can be bought as an investment or as a type of financial insurance.

When purchasing gold or silver as an investment the investor speculates that his purchase will grow in value. Usually he tries to buy when the metals are low and then sell them later when the prices rise. However, speculation in gold and other precious metals can be very risky as prices can rise and fall overnight, sometimes as much as one hundred dollars.

When someone buys gold or silver as insurance he is purchasing a safety measure against the ravages of inflation. These are sometimes referred to as "core holdings" which the buyer keeps in his own possession or in a safe deposit box at the bank. Normally these "core holdings" are purchased at the current price and never sold or traded unless the government reverses its monetary policy and accepts a gold standard or unless the economic system crashes and the holder is forced to use them as barter simply to survive.

Some experts suggest that a total of 30-50% of

a person's net worth or total investment portfolio include such precious metals as gold, silver, platinum and semi-numismatic (collector variety) coins. Gold should be bullion in the form of bars or coins. The U.S. Morgan Silver Dollar and the U.S. $20 Double Eagle Gold coins are deemed valuable for any portfolio. Before purchasing any precious metals we highly recommend that you contact someone you trust and who knows the market.

Mutual Funds

If you have only a minimal amount of money ($250-$500) to invest you will probably not be welcomed with open arms and smiling faces at your local bank. However, you can join with other small investors (large ones too) who pool their money together into a large fund managed by trained professionals. These we refer to as mutual funds.

Mutual funds are designed for wealth accumulation or for income purposes. When you choose a fund primarily for growth you attempt to protect your future from inflation. Usually you buy common stock in a business hoping your investment will significantly rise in value. When you pick a fund to experience immediate income you select safe, reasonably predictable investments which pay annual interest or dividends.

When you choose a mutual fund you receive the advantage of professional management, diversified securities, risk reduction, lower commissions, buying power, ease of liquidation, convenience, service and easier accounting of your investments. 18

Money Market Funds

A money market fund is a specific type of mutual fund pooling numerous investors together to invest billions of dollars on a short term basis for maximum safety and ease of liquidity. Money market funds enjoy the same advantages as other mutual funds.

When you buy into a money market you actually purchase shares in the fund and become one of its owners. As an owner-shareholder the earnings from your investment are technically dividends.

In a money market fund your dollars are used to purchase certificates of deposit, which are receipts for money loaned to banks; government securities, including Treasury Bills, Notes and Bonds; Federal Government loan guarantees such as Government National Mortgage Association (Ginnie Maes) and Federal Home Loan Mortgage Corporation (Freddie Mac); commercial paper, or loans issued by large corporations and banks; banker's acceptance notes, or promissory notes on import/export business; repos which are repurchase agreements; yankee dollars or certificates of deposit in a foreign bank and Eurodollars or money held on deposit in American banks located outside the United States. 19

IRAS

IRA stands for Individual Retirement Account

and provides an excellent investment for anyone who has earned income. Even if you have a retirement account where you work you can still open your own IRA, however, you will not be eligible for tax deductions on your contributions. IRAS provide an excellent, first time sampling of investing.

The practical advantages of owing an IRA are numerous. First of all you benefit from the boon of compound interest. Since IRÅS are intended for long term savings the interest you earn compounds and earns more interest over the years. For example if you deposited $10,000 compounded annually at 5% your investment would be worth $10,500 at the end of one year, $11,025 at the end of two years and by the end of the 25th year its value would climb to $33,864. Higher rates would of course bring greater returns.

Having an IRÅ allows you to defer the taxes on the accumulated interest earnings on your account until you begin to withdraw the funds after retirement. At this time you are more likely to fall in a lower tax bracket where the tax burden you bear will be considerably less. This means you will pay minimal taxes on the interest you earned from your IRA. A third advantage will be for those who are still eligible to deduct their contributions (up to $2,000) from their taxable income.

Finally, with an IRA you get the freedom to choose how and where you want your money invested. I recently opened an IRA that gives me the options to purchase Time Deposits, U.S. Government securities, stocks, bonds, mutual funds and precious metals. You also have the freedom to move your assets from one custodian to another without penalty. Possible custodians include banks, money market funds, brokerage firms, mutual funds, and insurance companies.

Stocks and Bonds

The practice of buying stock in a company has been around for a long time. When a person purchases available stock in any of the number of businesses listed on the various stock exchanges he actually buys a part or share in the company. Some companies hold millions of shares and when you own even a very minute portion of these shares you hold a corresponding portion of the company's equity.

In order to buy stock your purchase must be conducted through a stockbroker or licensed sales person. He in turn places your order with the stock exchange at the going rate for that day. The stock market operates on the principle of supply and demand. The more people want to purchase a particular stock the higher its value will be. When the stock is not in high demand its value will drop.

Playing the stock market is very much like gambling. You stand to lose your shirt if you are not careful. Normally it is recommended that anyone getting involved in the trading of stock should become well versed on how the stock market operates. Before investing in any particular company one should always read and study its annual report and prospectus to determine the company's worth, volume of debt, growth potential and management philosophy.

Also, check the growth of the stock. Is the value increasing over the years? What about the company's volatility? Has there been inconsistency in the company's performance? Does the company have a good price earnings ratio and does it pay dividends? These are all question that should be answered before giving any of your hard earned dollars to any business concern. A good friend told me that about 98% of those who dabble in the stock market end up losing money. Do your homework before and not after investing.

When you buy a bond you actually loan your money to a corporation. A bond is a long term debt security usually lasting from 5 to 30 years. Interest is paid to the investor until the maturity date of the bond. Your rate of interest does not fluctuate should the corporation's performance improve. If the company experiences hard times you will continue to receive your regular interest but if it goes belly up you could suffer the loss of your original investment.

Bob Madigan and Lawrence Kasoff suggest the consideration of four things when investing in bonds. First, what is the risk factor? "Some bonds are safer than others, while some are very risky." Second, what rate of return or earnings will you receive? "The return is what you receive either quarterly or upon maturity depending on the type of bond." Third, what is the average cost of your bonds? With bonds you purchase some investments "at higher prices and some at lower prices, thus averaging your overall purchase cost." Finally, when is the maturity or repayment date of your bond? "If you wait until the maturity date, you are guaranteed to get your principal back." [20] As in the purchase of stock, the investor should do all his homework before making his final investment decision.

<u>Giving</u>

Like the early church and the apostles we should be diligent in helping the poor and supporting those who labor in ministering and teaching the word of God (Gal 2:10, I Tim 5:17-18). In striving to get out of debt and in building up our economic worth we must not overlook these biblical mandates. We suggest that no matter what your current financial situation happens to be, you continue to pay your tithes and offerings to the work of God's kingdom.

The amount we give should be abundant and the tithe should be set as the minimum goal of our giving. Some, like the LeTourneaus, will be able to give more than 10% but none should give less. In extreme cases of debt a person may find it necessary to forego his giving temporarily but upon reducing his obligations he should return to giving his full tithe. It has taken some of us years to get into the financial mess we are in so we should not expect to be delivered from our economic woes over night. However, we should not neglect God's work because of our past financial blunders. Remember, God promises a blessing, not necessarily monetarily, to everyone who follows his instructions about giving to the poor and needy (II Cor 9:6-7, Deut 15:10).

Conclusion

For more than four decades our economic stability has declined. Savings has dropped from 25.2 percent of disposable income in 1944 to today's incredibly low rate of 2 percent. To turn these statistics around we must cut back on our indulgent life style, pay our debts, help the needy and begin investing in the future.

Home industries are becoming a national phenomenon. For whatever reason many Americans are discovering the value of investing in their own businesses. "Some are women wanting the privilege of raising their own children. Others are men who have given up the corporate rat race...Many are nurturing a part time solution to their financial problems. And some, as one home-worker put it, just want to be able to cut million-dollar deals over the phone while wearing their pajamas and bunny slippers." [21]

Husbands should take steps to become self employed and use their skills in a home business. The advantages of managing your own operation are conducive and can supply you many personal freedoms not available as another's employe. Other forms of investment include U.S. Government securities, precious metals, mutual funds, money market funds, iras, and stocks and bonds. Giving for God's work should take the highest priority in our investment goals. Charles Spurgeon, *"The Prince of Preachers,"* once taught:

"God's intent in endowing any person with more substance than he needs is that he may have the pleasurable office, or rather the delightful privilege, of relieving want and woe. Alas, how many there are who consider that store which God has put into their hands on purpose for the poor and needy, to be only so much provision for their excessive luxury, a luxury which pampers them but yields them neither benefit nor pleasure. Others dream that wealth is given them that they may keep it under lock and key, cankering and corroding, breeding covetousness and care. Who dares roll a stone over the well's mouth when thirst is raging all around? Who dares keep the bread from the women and children who are ready to gnaw their own arms for hunger? Above all, who dares allow the sufferer to writhe in agony uncared for, and the sick to pine into their graves unnursed? This is no small sin: it is a crime to be answered for, to the Judge, when He shall come to judge the quick and the dead."[22]

End Notes

Chapter One

1. Donald McAlvany, "The Coming Real Estate Bust," *The McAlvany Intelligence Advisor*, August 1989, p. 1. A monthly newsletter containing an analysis of economic, monetary and political trends. Explicitly Christian, conservative and free market in its perspective. Mr. McAlvany is President of International Collectors Associates, a precious metals brokerage and consultation firm.

2. Ron Blue, The Debt Squeeze (Pomona, California: Focus on the Family Publishing, 1989), p. 78.

3. Ibid., p. 2.

4. John J. Cunningham, How to Unscramble Your Nestegg (Denver, Colorado: Warrior Publishing, Inc., 1988), p. 36. The author, a former banker, offers sound advice on mortgage prepayment.

5. Howard Ruff, Making Money (New York: Simon and Schuster, 1984), p. 135. Mr. Ruff wrote this book as a guide to help middle class Americans make wise use of their money. He also produces the monthly newsletter, *The Financial Success Report*.

6. Judith Briles, <u>Faith and Savvy Too!</u> (Ventura, California: Regal Books, 1988), p. 92. This book is subtitled, *The Christian Woman's Guide to Money*. Unfortunately she fails to build her arguments in favor of debt from the scriptures. More than likely because the Bible does not support her position.

7. Ibid., p. 94.

8. Blue, p. 28.

9. Ibid., p. 28.

10. Ibid., p. 28.

11. Ruff, p. 135.

Chapter Two

1. Milton Lomask, <u>The Spirit of 1787: The Making of Our Constitution</u> (New York: Ballantine Books, 1980), p. 35. A very readable history of the making of our Constitution. The author covers the Critical Period of American history, the Federal Convention and the debates for ratification.

2. Ibid., p. 36.

3. Henry Steele Commager and Richard B. Morris, ed., <u>The Spirit of Seventy-Six: The Story of the American Revolution as told by Participants</u> (New York: Harper & Row, Publishers, 1967), p. 1283. A good compilation of original source documents telling the story of the Ameri-

can War for Independence.

    4. W.B. Allen, ed., <u>George Washington: A Collection</u> (Indianapolis: Liberty Classics, 1988), pp. 218-219. A fine collection of Washington's letters and speeches. This edition is still available from Liberty Press.

    5. Lomask, p. 38.

    6. Commager and Morris, p. 1283.

    7. Clarence Carson, <u>A Basic History of the United States: The Beginning of the Republic, 1775-1825, Vol.2</u> (Greenville, Alabama: American Textbook Committee, 1984), pp. 58-59. This basic History of the United States appears in five volumes, is reasonably priced and is written from a conservative perspective. Can be adapted for home schooling complete with teacher's guide.

    8. Commager and Morris, p. 1283.

    9. Carson, p. 75.

    10. Ibid., pp. 76-78.

    11. Davis Rich Dewey, <u>Financial History of The United States</u> (New York: Longmans, Green and Co., 1924), p. 36. The book covers U.S. financial history from colonial days through 1921.

    12. Ibid., p. 39.

    13. Ibid., p. 41.

14. Hans Sennholz, <u>Debts and Deficits</u> (Spring Mills, Pennsylvania: Libertarian Press, 1987), p. 147. Dr. Sennholz is head of the Department of Economics at Grove City College. He has written several books on monetary affairs. In an age of continuous inflation and big government debt this book is very important.

15. Ibid., p. 147.

16. S.C. Mooney, <u>Usury: Destroyer of Nations</u> (Warsaw, Ohio: A Theopolis Publication, 1988), p. 85. An extensive study on the teaching of usury throughout history. The author answers several excuses for its practice today.

17. William M. <u>Thayer, Gaining Favor With God and Man</u> (Portland, Oregon: Mantle Ministries, 1989), pp.26 & 27. Brief snapshots from the lives of great historical figures, known and unknown, fill the pages of this classic reprint. Geared to inspire youth.

18. Sennholz, pp. 75-77.

19. Ibid., p. 11.

20. Ibid., p. 11.

21. Ibid., p. 11.

22, Allen, p. 242.

23. Ibid., p. 244.

24. Sennholz, p. 71.

25. For a discussion of these vulnerabilities see: Hans Sennholz, <u>Debts and Deficits</u> (Spring Mills, Pennsylvania: Libertarian Press, 1987), pp. 147-161.

26. Allen, p. 522.

Chapter Three

1. Judith Briles, <u>Faith and Savvy Too!</u> (Ventura, California: Regal Books, 1988), p. 85.

2. Ibid., p. 85.

3. Ibid., p. 86.

4. Larry Burkett, <u>Your Finances in Changing Times</u> (Chicago: Moody Press, 1982), p. 56. This well known Christian financial advisor gives practical help on God's principles of personal finance.

5. Ron Blue, <u>Master Your Money</u> (Nashville, Tennessee: Thomas Nelson Publishers, 1986), p.55. Ron gives step-by-step advice on planning for financial freedom.

6. Merrill F. Unger & William White, Jr., Editors, <u>Nelson's Expository Dictionary of the Old Testament</u> (Nash-

ville: Thomas Nelson Publishers, 1980), p. 367.

7. Matthew Henry, *A Commentary on the Whole Bible: Volume 3, Job to Song of Solomon* (Iowa Falls, Iowa: World Bible Publishers, No Date), p. 917.

8. Matthew Poole, *A Commentary on the Holy Bible: Volume II: Psalms-Malachi* (McLean, Virginia: MacDonald Publishing Company, No Date), p. 257.

9. Arnold Dallimore, *George Whitefield, Volume 1* (Carlisle, Pennsylvania: The Banner of Truth Trust, 1975), p. 454. An excellent biography of Whitefield in two big volumes. The author shows how Whitefield was the actual founder of Methodism.

10. Ibid., p. 454.

11. Ibid., p. 582.

12. Ibid., pp. 584-585.

13. Ibid., p. 462.

14. Arnold Dallimore, *George Whitefield, Volume 2* (Westchester, Illinois: Crossway Books, 1983), p. 49.

15. Ibid., p. 218.

16. Ibid., p. 218.

17. Ibid., p. 219.

18. Ibid., p. 219.

19. Ibid., p. 219.

20. Ibid., p. 471.

21. Ibid., p. 403.

22. Ibid., p. 491.

23. Gary North, <u>Tools of Dominion</u> (Tyler, Texas: Institute for Christian Economics, 1990), p. 196. This book is the author's economic commentary on the case laws of Exodus. He refers to the book as a "fat book of social transformation." It contains 1,287 pages.

Chapter Four

1. Charles Ludwig, <u>Susanna Wesley</u> (Milford, Michigan: Mott Media, 1984), pp. 111-116. A good, readable biography of the mother of John and Charles Wesley. This book is part of the Sower Series biographies.

2. Ibid., pp. 116-117.

3. Ibid., p. 117.

4. Ibid., p. 118.

5. Ibid., pp. 131-137.

6. David Chilton, <u>Productive Christians in an Age of Guilt Manipula-</u>

tors (Tyler, Texas: Institute for Christian Economics, 1981), p. 223. This is the author's response to Ron Sider's book; *Rich Christians in an Age of Hunger*. If you have read Sider's book you owe it to yourself to read Chilton's response.

    7. Robert Alden, <u>Malachi: The Expositor's Bible Commentary: Volume 7</u> (Grand Rapids, Michigan: Zondervan Publishing House, 1985), p. 721.

    8. John Calvin, <u>Zechariah & Malachi</u> (Carlisle, Pennsylvania: The Banner of Truth Trust, 1986), p. 586.

    9. John MacArthur, <u>The MacArthur New Testament Commentary: Hebrews</u> (Chicago: Moody Press, 1983), p.375. This well known pastor-teacher has embarked upon the writing of a complete commentary on the New Testament. MacArthur's books are worth reading for their exegetical content.

    10. Ibid., p. 375.

    11. Ibid., p. 375.

    12. Ibid., p. 375.

    13. Ibid., p. 375.

    14. Ibid., p. 376.

    15. Tim LaHaye, <u>Faith of Our Founding Fathers</u> (Brentwood, Tennessee: Wolgemuth & Hyatt Publishers, 1987), p. 220.

This well known author gives evidence of the Christian influence on the founding of our nation.

16. T.R. Fehrenbach, Greatness to Spare (Princeton, New Jersey: D. Van Nostrand Company, 1968), p. 92. Brief lives of the men who signed the Declaration of Independence.

17. Ibid., p. 92.

18. Christopher Collier and James Lincoln Collier, Decision in Philadelphia (New York: Ballantine Books, 1986), p. 79. An exciting account of the Constitutional Convention of 1787.

19. Fehrenbach, p. 98.

20. Ibid., p. 99.

21. LaHaye, p. 221.

22. M.E. Bradford, A Worthy Company (Marlborough, New Hampshire: Plymouth Rock Foundation, 1982), p. 80. Bradford gives brief accounts of the lives of the men who framed the Constitution of the United States. The author gives the religious background of each delegate.

23. Fehrenbach, p. 101.

24. Herbert Schlossberg, Idols For Destruction (Nashville: Thomas Nelson Publishers, 1983), p. 89. The author analyzes American culture in the light of the biblical teachings on judgment and

idolatry. The cover of the book says "must reading for thinking Christians who refuse to be owned by any of the world's systems."

25. Charles Haddon Spurgeon, <u>Spurgeon's Sermons: Volume 6</u> (Grand Rapids, Michigan: Baker Book House, 1989), p. 127-128. A collection of the sermons of this great 19th century preacher.

26. W.E. Vine, <u>An Expository Dictionary of New Testament Words</u> (Old Tappan, New Jersey: Fleming H. Revell Company, 1940), p. 253.

27. Larry Burkett, <u>Your Finances in Changing Times</u> (Chicago: Moody Press, 1982), p.62. This well known Christian financial advisor gives practical help on God's principles of finance.

28. Jack B. Straus, Jr., <u>Financial Freedom</u> (Brentwood, Tennessee: Wolgemuth & Hyatt Publishers, 1988), p. 73-74. The author, a lawyer in Dallas Texas, gives his ideas on financial freedom. It is good to compare his thoughts with Burkett and Blue.

29. C.F. Keil and F. Delitzsch, <u>A Commentary on the Old Testament in Ten Volumes: Volume 6</u> (Grand Rapids, Michigan: William B. Eerdmans Publishing Company, 1975), p. 198.

30. Matthew Henry, <u>Commentary on the Whole Bible: Volume 6: Acts to Revelation</u> (Iowa Falls, Iowa: World Bible

Publishers, No Date), p. 992.

31. Ron Blue, The Debt Squeeze (Pomona, California: Focus on the Family Publishing, 1989), p. 38. Ron Blue offers advice in helping Christians live financially free. Easy to read style with numerous anecdotes.

32. Ibid., p. 47.

33. Larry Burkett, Debt-Free Living (Chicago: Moody Press, 1989), p. 56-57. Larry Burkett instructs the reader on how to get out of debt and stay out. The greatest value in this book is the fascinating stories of how numerous people got into debt and then by applying sound economic principles became financially free.

34. Blue, The Debt Squeeze, p. 45.

35. Ibid., p. 80.

36. Kenneth Wuest, Wuest's Word Studies From the Greek New Testament, Volume One (Grand Rapids, Michigan: Wm. B. Eerdmans Publishing Company, 1973), p. 227.

37. John Murray, The Epistle To The Romans (Grand Rapids, Michigan: Wm. B. Eerdmans Publishing Company, 1968), p. 158-159. Murray was a great teacher and scholar of the Reformed tradition. His writings are worth reading in an era when the church is engulfed in doctrinal compromise and worldly living.

Chapter Five

1. William Bradford, *Of Plymouth Plantation, 1620-1647* (New York: Alfred A. Knopf, 1970), p. 92. An original source document of the history of the Plymouth Colony. It is considered the first actual piece of American literature. Essential reading for every American.

2. Ibid., p. 93.

3. Peter Marshall and David Manuel, *The Light and the Glory* (Old Tappan, New Jersey: Fleming H. Revell Company, 1977), p. 138. An excellent account of American history from a Christian perspective. Recommended for all history buffs.

4. Ibid., p. 139.

5. Ibid., p. 139.

6. Tom Rose, *Economics: Principles and Policy from a Christian Perspective* (Mercer, Pennsylvania: American Enterprise Publications, 1986), p. 118. A good introduction into the world of economics. Topics include basic economics, the market system, distribution of income, and supply and demand. Also contains chapters on the nature of man and the Bible and economics.

7. Eugen von Bohm-Bawerk, *Capital and Interest; Volume 1* (Spring Mills, Pennsylvania: Libertarian Press, 1959),

p. 5. Bohm-Bawerk is an Austrian economist of the classical liberal tradition. This book is geared for the more serious economic student. It covers the history of interest and discusses in great detail the many theories of interest.

8. Rose, p. 119.

9. Ibid., p. 165.

10. Bettina B. Greaves, <u>Free Market Economics; A Syllabus</u> (Irvington-on-Hudson, New York: The Foundation For Economic Education, 1975), p. 232. The Foundation For Economic Education provides excellent material on the free market. Mrs. Greaves' book gives a good start for the one who is not familiar with the principles of free market economics. This book can easily be adapted for classroom use and home schooling at the high school level.

11. S.C. Mooney, <u>Usury; Destroyer of Nations</u> (Warsaw, Ohio: A Theopolis Publication, 1988), p. 22. To the writers knowledge this is the only book in print devoted entirely to the discussion of usury. It contains a lengthy history of usury practices and commentary on every verse from the Bible that deals with the topic.

12. James Strong, <u>Hebrew and Chaldee Dictionary Accompanying The Exhaustive Concordance</u> (Nashville, Tennessee: Crusade Bible Publishers, No Date), p. 81.

13. Ibid., p. 78.

14. Gary North, Tools of Dominion (Tyler, Texas: Institute for Christian Economics, 1990), pp. 710-711.

15. Ibid., p. 712.

16. Rose, p. 165-166.

17. Bohm-Bawerk, p. 10.

18. Quoted from S.C. Mooney, Usury: Destroyer of Nations, p.32.

19. Aristotle, The Politics (Great Britain: Penguin Books, 1962), p. 87. A classic in the study of political science and government. Our founding fathers were well versed on the works of Plato and Aristotle.

20. Bohm-Bawerk, p. 11.

21. Will Durant, Caesar and Christ (New York: Simon and Schuster, 1944), p. 79. A highly acclaimed history of civilization. This is volume three of eleven volumes.

22. Ibid., p. 88.

23. Ibid., p. 129.

24. Ibid., p. 130.

25. Bohm-Bawerk, p. 11.

26. Alfred Edersheim, The Life and Times of Jesus the Messiah Volume II (Grand Rapids, Michigan: Wm B. Eerdmans Publishing Company, 1959), p. 459. A classic work on the life and times of Christ. Includes pertinent cultural and historic information useful to the reader.

27. John MacArthur, Jr., The MacArthur New Testament Commentary: Matthew 24-28 (Chicago: Moody Press, 1989), p. 100.

28. Ibid., p. 99.

29. Edersheim, p. 464.

30. Ibid., p. 464.

31. Flavius Josephus, The Works of Josephus, trans. William Whiston, A.M. (Peabody, Mass: Hendrickson Publishers, 1987), p. 121. A complete and unabridged one volume edition of this classic in Jewish history. Josephus provides us with indispensable information regarding our understanding of Jewish thought, culture, background and history in the times of Christ and the apostles.

32. Joachim Jeremias, Jerusalem in the Time of Jesus (Philadelphia: Fortress Press, 1969), p. 310.

33. Ibid., p. 311.

34. Alfred Edersheim, Sketches of

Jewish Social Life in the Days of Christ (Grand Rapids, Michigan: Wm. B. Eerdmans Publishing Co., 1988), p. 211. A good presentation of the social life of Palestine during the time of Christ.

Chapter Six

1. Charles Spurgeon, _C.H. Spurgeon: The Early Years 1834-1859_ (London: The Banner of Truth Trust, 1967), pp. 23-24. This is a revised edition of Spurgeon's autobiography, originally compiled by his wife and private secretary. The complete account of Spurgeon's experience with debt is contained in the above pages. An excellent account of this noted 19th century preacher.

2. Dr. Tim Dowley, Organizing Editor, _Eerdman's Handbook to The History of Christianity_ (Grand Rapids, Michigan: Wm. B. Eerdman's Publishing Company, 1977), p. 102-103. A brief history of the church complete with photographs and special articles.

3. The Rev. Alexander Roberts and James Donaldson, Editors, _The Ante-Nicene Fathers; Volume III, Latin Christianity: Its Founder, Tertullian_ (Grand Rapids, Michigan: Wm. B. Eerdmans Publishing Company, 1989), p. 270. A lengthy edition of the writings of Tertullian including his apologetic, treatise against Marcion and ethical writings.

4. Ibid., p. 345.

5. Ibid., p. 372-373.

6. Durant, p. 656-657. For a more detailed description of the triumph of Christianity during the reign of Constantine see Eusebius' <u>The History of the Church from Christ to Constantine.</u>

7. Ibid., p. 657.

8. Ibid., p. 658-661.

9. Henry R. Percival, Editor, <u>Nicene and Post-Nicene Fathers of the Christian Church: Volume XIV; The Seven Ecumenical Councils of the Undivided Church: Their Canons and Dogmatic Decrees</u> (Grand Rapids, Michigan: Wm. B. Eerdmans Publishing Company, 1956), p. 36. A full and complete compilation of the first seven church councils. Includes editorial comments.

10. Ibid., p. 36.

11. Ibid., p. 36.

12. Charles White, J. Randall Petersen, and Daniel V. Runyon, Editors, "Gallery of Church Fathers and Their Thoughts on Wealth," <u>Christian History</u>, Volume VI, No. 2, 11. Christian History Magazine provides good, brief historical data on the lives of Christians from a bygone era. Some issues cover topics which have confronted the church for centuries.

13. Philip Schaff and Henry Wace, Editors, Nicene and Post-Nicene Fathers of the Christian Church; Volume VIII, St. Basil, trans. The Rev. Blomfield Jackson, M.A. (Grand Rapids, Michigan: Wm. B. Eerdmans Publishing Company, 1989), p. 228. A thorough collection of Basil's writings including his work on the Holy Spirit.

14. Charles White, p. 35.

15. Keith Yandell, "The City of God: Augustine's Timeless Classic About the Timeless City," Christian History, Volume VI, No. 3, 22. This issue of Christian History is dedicated entirely to Augustine. Back issues are available from the publisher.

16. Saint Augustine, The City of God, trans. Marcus Dods, D.D. (New York: The Modern Library, 1950), p. 91. A complete and unabridged edition of the Christian classic.

17. Ibid., p. 91.

18. Percival, p.445.

19. Ibid., p. 369.

20. Mooney, p. 42-43.

21. Charles White, J. Randall Petersen, and Daniel V. Runyon, Editors, "From the Archives," Christian History, Volume VI, No. 2, 24.

22. Ibid., p. 24.

23. Ibid., p. 24.

24. Bohm-Bawerk, p. 17-18.

25. Fernand Braudel, *Civilization and Capitalism, 15th - 18th Century, Volume II, The Wheels of Commerce* (New York: Harper & Row Publishers, 1979), p. 563. This is volume two of a three volume set on social and economic history from the Middle Ages to the Industrial Revolution.

26. Bohm-Bawerk, p. 18.

27. Ibid., p. 18.

28. Roland H. Bainton, *Here I Stand; A Life of Martin Luther,* (New York: Abingdon-Cokesbury Press, No Date), p. 237. A standard work on the life of Luther. Still available from your favorite Christian book distributor.

29. Martin Luther, *Luther's Works, Volume 9, Lectures on Deuteronomy*, trans. Richard R. Caemmerer (Saint Louis: Concordia Publishing House, 1960), p. 234. This American Edition of Luther's multi-volume work is very extensive. Recommended for anyone interested in Luther's writings.

30. Ibid., p. 146.

31. John Calvin, *Commentaries on the First Twenty Chapters of the Book of*

the Prophet Ezekiel, trans. Thomas Myers, (Grand Rapids, Michigan: Baker Book House, No Date), p. 225. Calvin was a prolific writer and wrote a commentary on almost every book of the Bible. This edition by Baker is a complete set of his commentaries.

32. Ibid., p. 227.

33. Ibid., p. 226-227.

34. David Hume, The History of England, Volume IV (Indianapolis: Liberty Press/Liberty Classics, 1983), p. 379-380. Originally written in the 18th century, this edition is based on the 1778 edition with the author's last corrections and improvements. On page 380 Hume notes that "an act passed in 1571, violently condemns all usury; but permits ten percent interest to be payed" illustrating the fact that men began to change their thinking and differentiate between usury (high interest rates) and interest (legal interest rates).

35. Calvin, p. 228.

36. Allen O. Miller, M. Eugene Osterhaven, Aladar Komjathy, and James I. McCord, The Heidelberg Catechism with Commentary (Philadelphia: United Church Press, 1962), p. 5. This edition of the Catechism is a new modern translation and may contain some modified terminology.

37. Zacharias Ursinus, The Commentary of Dr. Zacharias Ursinus on the

G.W. Williard, A.M. (Columbus: Scott & Bascom Printers, 1852), p. 595. An in depth commentary on the Heidelberg Catechism by its author. As an interesting side note, the modern version (see note 36) uses the words "exorbitant interest" instead of the word "usury" as used in the older text.

38. Ibid., p. 597.

39. Leland Ryken, Worldly Saints: The Puritans As They Really Were (Grand Rapids, Michigan: Zondervan Publishing House, 1986), p. 67. An excellent, well documented book on the Puritan life style.

40. Thomas Watson, Body of Divinity (Grand Rapids, Michigan: Baker Book House, 1979), p. 342. An exhaustive study of Watson's sermons on the Westminster Shorter Catechism. Excellent material!

41. Bohm-Bawerk, p. 22-25.

42. Ibid., p. 25-27.

43. Ibid., p. 27-30.

44. William Greider, Secrets of the Temple: How the Federal Reserve Runs the Country (New York: Simon & Schuster, 1989), p. 176.

45. Ibid., p. 175.

46. Ibid., p. 175.

Chapter Seven

1. Ron Blue, The Debt Squeeze (Pomona, California: Focus on the Family Publishing, 1989), p. 121.

2. George and Marjean Fooshee, You Can Beat the Money Squeeze (Old Tappan, New Jersey: Fleming H. Revell Company, 1980). p. 66. The Fooshees offer families financial advice from a biblical perspective.

3. Blue, p. 81.

4. Marc Eisenson, A Banker's Secret (Elizaville, New York: Good Advice Press, 1989), p. 213. A how to book on prepaying your loans. This book contains numerous charts for the interested reader.

5. Cunningham, p. 56.

6. Ibid., p. 66.

7. We will produce a repayment schedule for interested readers for the modest price of $10.00 plus $2.00 for shipping. Order from Back Home Industries, P.O. Box 22495, Milwaukie, Oregon, 97222. Please include 1) the original loan amount, 2) the interest rate, 3) current loan balance, 4) term: original length of the loan in years, 5) monthly payment (minus any taxes & insurance included in your mortgage payment), 6) the amount of extra pre-payment you wish to add.

8. Cunningham, p. 126.

9. Ibid., p. 127.

10. Ibid., p. 127.

Chapter Eight

1. Burt Folsom, <u>John D. Rockefeller and the Oil Industry</u>, *The Freeman*, October, 1988, p. 402. The *Freeman* is a monthly publication produced by The Foundation For Economic Education. It adheres to the principles of private property, limited government and the free market.

2. Ibid., p. 404.

3. Ibid., p. 411.

4. William M. Thayer, <u>Gaining Favor With God and Man</u> (Portland, Oregon: Mantle Ministries, 1989), p. 246.

5. Ibid., p. 246.

6. Ibid., p. 246.

7. Ibid., p. 246.

8. Keynesian economics is named after John Maynard Kenynes the British born economist who's hatred of the free market and his love for a state controlled planning system permeated his writings. Keynes was a practicing homosexual of the most debauched variety.

Based on his life style, Keynes believed that "in the long run, we are all dead." Because of his perverted world view (homosexuality as a matter of preference) Keynes' outlook on life was short sighted. He had no posterity to care for and believed that saving for the future deserved great condemnation. The interested reader should study Ian Hodge's book, <u>Baptized Inflation</u> (Institute for Christian Economics, Tyler, Texas, 1986) for a better understanding of the Keynesian fallacies.

9. Henry Hazlitt, <u>The Failure of the "New Economics"</u> (Lanham, Maryland: University Press of America, 1983), p. 127. Mr. Hazlitt, one time columnist for Newsweek and The New York Times, analyzes the errors of Keynesian economics.

10. Ibid., p. 113.

11. John Cunningham, <u>How to Unscramble Your Nestegg</u>, p. 14.

12. Bettina B. Greaves, <u>Free Market Economics</u>, p. 235.

13. Charles Bridges, <u>A Commentary on Proverbs</u> (Carlisle, Pennsylvania: The Banner of Truth Trust, 1968), p. 623. Charles Bridges lived from 1794-1869 and was vicar of Old Newton, Suffolk from 1823-1849. This commentary on the book of Proverbs is considered one of his best works.

14. George and Marjean Foshee, <u>You

Can Beat the Money Squeeze (Old Tappan, New Jersey: Fleming H. Revell Company, 1980), p. 105.

15. Mary LaGrand Bouma, The Creative Homemaker (Minneapolis, Minnesota: Bethany Fellowship, 1973), pp. 98-99. This book raises a firm feminine voice in favor of marriage and homemaking.

16. Blue, The Debt Squeeze, p. 64.

17. Howard L. Dayton, Jr., Getting Out of Debt (Wheaton, Illinois: Tyndale House Publishers, 1986), p. 60.

18. Blue, p. 96.

19. Ibid., p. 96.

20. Wanda Sanseri, God's Priceless Woman (Milwaukie, Oregon: Back Home Industries 1991), pp. 137-138. Wanda gives women good, sound teaching on their role and place in society, home and church.

21. Ibid., p. 138.

22. E. Calvin Beisner, Prosperity and Poverty (Westchester, Illinois: Crossway Books, 1988), p. 206. Mr. Beisner is National Chairman of the Economics Committee of The Coalition on Revival. This book "offers clear teaching on Biblical principles of stewardship and economics, enabling us to make informed choices in these areas."

23. Ibid., p. 206.

Chapter Nine

1. Donald F. Ackland, *Moving Heaven and Earth: The Story of R.G. LeTourneau* (New York: The Iverson-Ford Associates, 1949), p. 155. The biography of the man who built heavy, land moving equip-ment and gave most of his income to Christian work.

2. Ibid., pp. 38-41.

3. Ibid., pp. 41-43.

4. Ibid., p. 59.

5. Ibid., p. 62.

6. Ibid., p. 73.

7. R.G. LeTourneau, *Mover of Men and Mountains* (Chicago: Moody Press, 1967), p. 279. This information was taken from the epilogue of the 1967 edition of LeTourneau's autobiography. It was written by Nels E. Stjernstrom.

8. Ibid., p. 280.

9. Ackland, p. 156.

10. Paul and Sarah Edwards, *Working From Home* (Los Angeles:Jeremy P. Tarcher, Inc., 1985), p. 7. The authors present numerous ideas and suggestions for helping your home business survive and grow. The sub-title for this book reads, "Everything you need to know about living and working under the same roof."

11. Barbara Brabec, <u>Homemade Money</u> (White Hall, Virginia: Betterway Publications, Inc., 1989), p. 17. A detailed book on getting into the home business industry. Highly recommended for the reader who is serious about working from the home.

12. Those interested in knowing more about these types of investments should read Arnold Corrigan & Phyllis C. Kaufman's, <u>Undrestanding Treasury Bills and other U.S. Government Securities</u> (Longmeadow Press, 1987). This is a simple guide on how the United States deficit can work for you.

13. Clarence Carson, <u>Basic Economics</u> (Wadley, Alabama: American Textbook Committee, 1988), p. 100. The author has written several books on economics from a free market point of view and also a complete, five volume, history of the United States. His books are worth reading for his insights on the ideas of liberty throughout history. Write to The Foundation for Economic Education, 30 S. Broadway, Irvington-on-Hudson, NY, 10533.

14. Ibid., p. 101.

15. Andrew Dickson White, <u>Fiat Money Inflation in France</u> (Irvington-on-Hudson, New York: The Foundation for Economic Education), p.100. The author was the founder of Cornell University in Ithaca, New York. This book, born from his lectures on the French Revolution, is

a classic on the ravages of fiat money schemes concocted by government.

16. Ibid., p. 104.

17. Rep. Ron Paul and Lewis Lehrman, *The Case For Gold* (Washington D.C.: Cato Institute, 1982), p. i. The authors, proponents of the gold standard, make a strong plea for monetary reform.

18. The reader interested in learning more about mutual funds is encouraged to read Arnold Corrigan and Phyllis Kaufman, *Understanding Mutual Funds* (Longmeadow Press, 1984).

19. Bob Madigan and Lawrence Kasoff, *The First-Time Investor* (New York: Prentice Hall Press, 1987), p. 42-43. A helpful introduction for the novice who wants to enter into the world of investment.

20. Ibid., p. 131-135.

21. Lindsey O'Connor, *Working At Home* (Eugene, Oregon: Harvest House, 1990), p. 9. The author shows how you can make your dream of working at home become a reality.

22. C.H. Spurgeon, *Metropolitan Tabernacle Pulpit, Volume 23* (London, UK: Passmore and Alabaster, 1877), p. 353. Quoted from George Grant, *Bringing in the Sheaves* (Atlanta, Georgia: American Vision Press, 1985), p. 66.

Appendix A
Scripture Index

	Page
Exodus	
14:13	46
20:21	61
22:25-27	43,54,60,66
Leviticus	
25:35	61
25:35-38	43,54,55,60,66
Deuteronomy	
8:18	47
15:10	138
15:1-11	43-44,61,66
23:19	60,66,84
23:20	61,66
24:10-13	43,54,55,60,66
Joshua	
7:10-26 (especially vs. 21)	51
I Samuel	
2:7	48
Nehemiah	
5:1-13	62

Psalms	Page
15:5	61
37:21	38
112:5	44

Proverbs	
5:15-20	111
6:24-29	111
15:16	45,72
19:17	44
22:7	31,33,34
27:1	52
28:8	62
31:10-31	111-113

Ecclesiastes	
5:10	46

Ezekiel	
18:4-13	62
18:5-9	84
18:7,12	55,60

Malachi	
3:8	42-43

Matthew	
5:38-42	65
6:12	32
6:19-21	48
6:24	48
6:31-33	46-47

Matthew (Continued)	Page
18:21-35	35
19:16-23	49
25:27	67-71
28:20	121

Mark	
10:21	48

Luke	
6:34	65
6:34-36	54,78
6:35	66
7:6	47
9:57-62	35
12:15	50
16:19-31	49

John	
14:15,21	121

Acts	
4:32	77
4:34-35	77-78
14:8-20	47

Romans	
1:14	32
8:12	32
8:28	46
13:8	31,38,39, 55-56

	Page
I Corinthians	
7:17-27	34
7:21	39
II Corinthians	
9:6-7	138
Galatians	
2:10	138
5:3	32
6:7	31,85
Ephesians	
1:11	48
3:8	48
Philippians	
2:20	48
4:19	56
Colossians	
3:2	48
I Timothy	
5:17-18	138
5:8	44
6:6	45
6:6-8	45
6:9-10	46
6:17	47

	Page
Titus	
2:4-5	111
Philemon	
8-22	35
Hebrews	
13:5	45
James	
2:1-7	49
4:13-15	53
II Peter	
2:18-19	33
I John	
2:1-4	121

Mortgage Loan Account Information

Name: **Gary Sanseri**
Address: **8431 S.E. 36th Ave**
City, State ZIP: **Portland, OR 97222**
Telephone: **503-654-2300**
Reference: **Loan No. 50637**

Mortgage Data

Original Mortgage Amount:	85000.00
Annual Interest Rate (%):	9.00
Mortgage Period - Months:	360
Payments first (1)/end (0) of mo:	0
Month and year (xx.yy) of first payment:	1.91
Monthly Mortgage Payment:	683.93
Total Interest:	161214.52
Total Payments:	246214.52

sample amortization schedule

Payment			For this Month			Cumulative		
No.	Mo.	Yr.	Interest	Principal	Balance	Interest	Principal	Int. for Yr.
1	1	91	637.50	46.43	84953.57	637.50	46.43	637.50
2	2	91	637.15	46.78	84906.79	1274.65	93.21	1274.65
3	3	91	636.80	47.13	84859.67	1911.45	140.33	1911.45
4	4	91	636.45	47.48	84812.18	2547.90	187.82	2547.90
5	5	91	636.09	47.84	84764.35	3183.99	235.65	3183.99
6	6	91	635.73	48.20	84716.15	3819.72	283.85	3819.72
7	7	91	635.37	48.56	84667.59	4455.10	332.41	4455.10
8	8	91	635.01	48.92	84618.67	5090.10	381.33	5090.10
9	9	91	634.64	49.29	84569.38	5724.74	430.62	5724.74
10	10	91	634.27	49.66	84519.72	6359.01	480.28	6359.01
11	11	91	633.90	50.03	84469.69	6992.91	530.31	6992.91
12	12	91	633.52	50.41	84419.28	7626.43	580.72	7626.43
13	1	92	633.14	50.78	84368.50	8259.58	631.50	633.14
14	2	92	632.76	51.17	84317.33	8892.34	682.67	1265.91
15	3	92	632.38	51.55	84265.78	9524.72	734.22	1898.29
16	4	92	631.99	51.94	84213.85	10156.71	786.15	2530.28
17	5	92	631.60	52.33	84161.52	10788.32	838.48	3161.89
18	6	92	631.21	52.72	84108.80	11419.53	891.20	3793.10
19	7	92	630.82	53.11	84055.69	12050.35	944.31	4423.91
20	8	92	630.42	53.51	84002.18	12680.76	997.82	5054.33
21	9	92	630.02	53.91	83948.27	13310.78	1051.73	5684.35
22	10	92	629.61	54.32	83893.95	13940.39	1106.05	6313.96
23	11	92	629.20	54.72	83839.22	14569.60	1160.78	6943.16
24	12	92	628.79	55.14	83784.09	15198.39	1215.91	7571.96
25	1	93	628.38	55.55	83728.54	15826.77	1271.46	628.38
26	2	93	627.96	55.97	83672.58	16454.74	1327.42	1256.34

Payment			For this Month			Cumulative		
No.	Mo.	Yr.	Interest	Principal	Balance	Interest	Principal	Int. for Yr.
27	3	93	627.54	56.38	83616.19	17082.28	1383.81	1883.89
28	4	93	627.12	56.81	83559.38	17709.40	1440.62	2511.01
29	5	93	626.70	57.23	83502.15	18336.10	1497.85	3137.71
30	6	93	626.27	57.66	83444.49	18962.36	1555.51	3763.97
31	7	93	625.83	58.10	83386.39	19588.20	1613.61	4389.81
32	8	93	625.40	58.53	83327.86	20213.59	1672.14	5015.20
33	9	93	624.96	58.97	83268.89	20838.55	1731.11	5640.16
34	10	93	624.52	59.41	83209.48	21463.07	1790.52	6264.68
35	11	93	624.07	59.86	83149.62	22087.14	1850.38	6888.75
36	12	93	623.62	60.31	83089.31	22710.76	1910.69	7512.37
37	1	94	623.17	60.76	83028.55	23333.93	1971.45	623.17
38	2	94	622.71	61.22	82967.34	23956.65	2032.66	1245.88
39	3	94	622.26	61.67	82905.66	24578.90	2094.34	1868.14
40	4	94	621.79	62.14	82843.53	25200.69	2156.47	2489.93
41	5	94	621.33	62.60	82780.92	25822.02	2219.08	3111.26
42	6	94	620.86	63.07	82717.85	26442.88	2282.15	3732.11
43	7	94	620.38	63.55	82654.31	27063.26	2345.69	4352.50
44	8	94	619.91	64.02	82590.28	27683.17	2409.72	4972.41
45	9	94	619.43	64.50	82525.78	28302.60	2474.22	5591.83
46	10	94	618.94	64.99	82460.80	28921.54	2539.20	6210.78
47	11	94	618.46	65.47	82395.32	29540.00	2604.68	6829.23
48	12	94	617.96	65.96	82329.36	30157.96	2670.64	7447.20
49	1	95	617.47	66.46	82262.90	30775.43	2737.10	617.47
50	2	95	616.97	66.96	82195.94	31392.40	2804.06	1234.44
51	3	95	616.47	67.46	82128.48	32008.87	2871.52	1850.91
52	4	95	615.96	67.97	82060.52	32624.84	2939.48	2466.88
53	5	95	615.45	68.48	81992.04	33240.29	3007.96	3082.33
54	6	95	614.94	68.99	81923.05	33855.23	3076.95	3697.27
55	7	95	614.42	69.51	81853.55	34469.65	3146.45	4311.69
56	8	95	613.90	70.03	81783.52	35083.55	3216.48	4925.59
57	9	95	613.38	70.55	81712.97	35696.93	3287.03	5538.97
58	10	95	612.85	71.08	81641.88	36309.78	3358.12	6151.82
59	11	95	612.31	71.62	81570.27	36922.09	3429.73	6764.13
60	12	95	611.78	72.15	81498.12	37533.87	3501.88	7375.91
61	1	96	611.24	72.69	81425.42	38145.11	3574.58	611.24
62	2	96	610.69	73.24	81352.18	38755.80	3647.82	1221.93
63	3	96	610.14	73.79	81278.40	39365.94	3721.60	1832.07
64	4	96	609.59	74.34	81204.05	39975.53	3795.95	2441.66
65	5	96	609.03	74.90	81129.16	40584.56	3870.84	3050.69
66	6	96	608.47	75.46	81053.70	41193.02	3946.30	3659.15
67	7	96	607.90	76.03	80977.67	41800.93	4022.33	4267.06
68	8	96	607.33	76.60	80901.07	42408.26	4098.93	4874.39
69	9	96	606.76	77.17	80823.90	43015.02	4176.10	5481.15
70	10	96	606.18	77.75	80746.15	43621.20	4253.85	6087.33
71	11	96	605.60	78.33	80667.82	44226.79	4332.18	6692.92
72	12	96	605.01	78.92	80588.90	44831.80	4411.10	7297.93

Payment			For this Month			Cumulative		
No.	Mo.	Yr.	Interest	Principal	Balance	Interest	Principal	Int. for Yr.
73	1	97	604.42	79.51	80509.38	45436.22	4490.62	604.42
74	2	97	603.82	80.11	80429.28	46040.04	4570.72	1208.24
75	3	97	603.22	80.71	80348.57	46643.26	4651.43	1811.46
76	4	97	602.61	81.31	80267.25	47245.87	4732.75	2414.07
77	5	97	602.00	81.92	80185.33	47847.88	4814.67	3016.08
78	6	97	601.39	82.54	80102.79	48449.27	4897.21	3617.47
79	7	97	600.77	83.16	80019.63	49050.04	4980.37	4218.24
80	8	97	600.15	83.78	79935.85	49650.18	5064.15	4818.38
81	9	97	599.52	84.41	79851.44	50249.70	5148.56	5417.90
82	10	97	598.89	85.04	79766.39	50848.59	5233.61	6016.79
83	11	97	598.25	85.68	79680.71	51446.84	5319.29	6615.04
84	12	97	597.61	86.32	79594.39	52044.44	5405.61	7212.64
85	1	98	596.96	86.97	79507.42	52641.40	5492.58	596.96
86	2	98	596.31	87.62	79419.79	53237.71	5580.21	1193.26
87	3	98	595.65	88.28	79331.51	53833.35	5668.49	1788.91
88	4	98	594.99	88.94	79242.57	54428.34	5757.43	2383.90
89	5	98	594.32	89.61	79152.96	55022.66	5847.04	2978.22
90	6	98	593.65	90.28	79062.68	55616.31	5937.32	3571.86
91	7	98	592.97	90.96	78971.72	56209.28	6028.28	4164.83
92	8	98	592.29	91.64	78880.08	56801.57	6119.92	4757.12
93	9	98	591.60	92.33	78787.75	57393.17	6212.25	5348.72
94	10	98	590.91	93.02	78694.73	57984.07	6305.27	5939.63
95	11	98	590.21	93.72	78601.01	58574.28	6398.99	6529.84
96	12	98	589.51	94.42	78506.59	59163.79	6493.41	7119.35
97	1	99	588.80	95.13	78411.46	59752.59	6588.54	588.80
98	2	99	588.09	95.84	78315.61	60340.68	6684.39	1176.89
99	3	99	587.37	96.56	78219.05	60928.04	6780.95	1764.25
100	4	99	586.64	97.29	78121.77	61514.69	6878.23	2350.90
101	5	99	585.91	98.02	78023.75	62100.60	6976.25	2936.81
102	6	99	585.18	98.75	77925.00	62685.78	7075.00	3521.99
103	7	99	584.44	99.49	77825.51	63270.22	7174.49	4106.42
104	8	99	583.69	100.24	77725.27	63853.91	7274.73	4690.12
105	9	99	582.94	100.99	77624.28	64436.85	7375.72	5273.05
106	10	99	582.18	101.75	77522.53	65019.03	7477.47	5855.24
107	11	99	581.42	102.51	77420.02	65600.45	7579.98	6436.66
108	12	99	580.65	103.28	77316.74	66181.10	7683.26	7017.31
109	1	0	579.88	104.05	77212.69	66760.97	7787.31	579.88
110	2	0	579.10	104.83	77107.85	67340.07	7892.15	1158.97
111	3	0	578.31	105.62	77002.23	67918.38	7997.77	1737.28
112	4	0	577.52	106.41	76895.82	68495.89	8104.18	2314.80
113	5	0	576.72	107.21	76788.61	69072.61	8211.39	2891.52
114	6	0	575.91	108.01	76680.60	69648.53	8319.40	3467.43
115	7	0	575.10	108.82	76571.77	70223.63	8428.23	4042.53
116	8	0	574.29	109.64	76462.13	70797.92	8537.87	4616.82
117	9	0	573.47	110.46	76351.67	71371.39	8648.33	5190.29
118	10	0	572.64	111.29	76240.38	71944.02	8759.62	5762.93

Payment			For this Month			Cumulative		
No.	Mo.	Yr.	Interest	Principal	Balance	Interest	Principal	Int. for Yr.
119	11	0	571.80	112.13	76128.25	72515.83	8871.75	6334.73
120	12	0	570.96	112.97	76015.28	73086.79	8984.72	6905.69
121	1	1	570.11	113.81	75901.47	73656.90	9098.53	570.11
122	2	1	569.26	114.67	75786.80	74226.16	9213.20	1139.38
123	3	1	568.40	115.53	75671.27	74794.57	9328.73	1707.78
124	4	1	567.53	116.39	75554.88	75362.10	9445.12	2275.31
125	5	1	566.66	117.27	75437.61	75928.76	9562.39	2841.97
126	6	1	565.78	118.15	75319.46	76494.54	9680.54	3407.75
127	7	1	564.90	119.03	75200.43	77059.44	9799.57	3972.65
128	8	1	564.00	119.93	75080.50	77623.44	9919.50	4536.65
129	9	1	563.10	120.83	74959.68	78186.55	10040.32	5099.76
130	10	1	562.20	121.73	74837.95	78748.74	10162.05	5661.96
131	11	1	561.28	122.64	74715.30	79310.03	10284.70	6223.24
132	12	1	560.36	123.56	74591.74	79870.39	10408.26	6783.60
133	1	2	559.44	124.49	74467.24	80429.83	10532.76	559.44
134	2	2	558.50	125.42	74341.82	80988.34	10658.18	1117.94
135	3	2	557.56	126.37	74215.45	81545.90	10784.55	1675.51
136	4	2	556.62	127.31	74088.14	82102.52	10911.86	2232.12
137	5	2	555.66	128.27	73959.87	82658.18	11040.13	2787.78
138	6	2	554.70	129.23	73830.64	83212.88	11169.36	3342.48
139	7	2	553.73	130.20	73700.44	83766.61	11299.56	3896.21
140	8	2	552.75	131.18	73569.27	84319.36	11430.73	4448.97
141	9	2	551.77	132.16	73437.11	84871.13	11562.89	5000.73
142	10	2	550.78	133.15	73303.96	85421.91	11696.04	5551.51
143	11	2	549.78	134.15	73169.81	85971.69	11830.19	6101.29
144	12	2	548.77	135.16	73034.65	86520.46	11965.35	6650.07
145	1	3	547.76	136.17	72898.48	87068.22	12101.52	547.76
146	2	3	546.74	137.19	72761.29	87614.96	12238.71	1094.50
147	3	3	545.71	138.22	72623.07	88160.67	12376.93	1640.21
148	4	3	544.67	139.26	72483.82	88705.34	12516.18	2184.88
149	5	3	543.63	140.30	72343.52	89248.97	12656.48	2728.51
150	6	3	542.58	141.35	72202.16	89791.55	12797.84	3271.09
151	7	3	541.52	142.41	72059.75	90333.06	12940.25	3812.60
152	8	3	540.45	143.48	71916.27	90873.51	13083.73	4353.05
153	9	3	539.37	144.56	71771.71	91412.88	13228.29	4892.42
154	10	3	538.29	145.64	71626.07	91951.17	13373.93	5430.71
155	11	3	537.20	146.73	71479.34	92488.37	13520.66	5967.91
156	12	3	536.10	147.83	71331.50	93024.46	13668.50	6504.00
157	1	4	534.99	148.94	71182.56	93559.45	13817.44	534.99
158	2	4	533.87	150.06	71032.50	94093.32	13967.50	1068.86
159	3	4	532.74	151.19	70881.31	94626.06	14118.69	1601.60
160	4	4	531.61	152.32	70728.99	95157.67	14271.01	2133.21
161	5	4	530.47	153.46	70575.53	95688.14	14424.47	2663.68
162	6	4	529.32	154.61	70420.92	96217.45	14579.08	3192.99
163	7	4	528.16	155.77	70265.15	96745.61	14734.85	3721.15
164	8	4	526.99	156.94	70108.21	97272.60	14891.79	4248.14

Payment			For this Month			Cumulative		
No.	Mo.	Yr.	Interest	Principal	Balance	Interest	Principal	Int. for Yr.
165	9	4	525.81	158.12	69950.09	97798.41	15049.91	4773.95
166	10	4	524.63	159.30	69790.79	98323.04	15209.21	5298.58
167	11	4	523.43	160.50	69630.29	98846.47	15369.71	5822.01
168	12	4	522.23	161.70	69468.59	99368.69	15531.41	6344.23
169	1	5	521.01	162.91	69305.67	99889.71	15694.33	521.01
170	2	5	519.79	164.14	69141.53	100409.50	15858.47	1040.81
171	3	5	518.56	165.37	68976.17	100928.06	16023.83	1559.37
172	4	5	517.32	166.61	68809.56	101445.38	16190.44	2076.69
173	5	5	516.07	167.86	68641.70	101961.46	16358.30	2592.76
174	6	5	514.81	169.12	68472.58	102476.27	16527.42	3107.57
175	7	5	513.54	170.38	68302.20	102989.81	16697.80	3621.12
176	8	5	512.27	171.66	68130.54	103502.08	16869.46	4133.38
177	9	5	510.98	172.95	67957.59	104013.06	17042.41	4644.36
178	10	5	509.68	174.25	67783.34	104522.74	17216.66	5154.05
179	11	5	508.38	175.55	67607.78	105031.12	17392.22	5662.42
180	12	5	507.06	176.87	67430.91	105538.17	17569.09	6169.48
181	1	6	505.73	178.20	67252.72	106043.91	17747.28	505.73
182	2	6	504.40	179.53	67073.18	106548.30	17926.82	1010.13
183	3	6	503.05	180.88	66892.30	107051.35	18107.70	1513.18
184	4	6	501.69	182.24	66710.07	107553.04	18289.93	2014.87
185	5	6	500.33	183.60	66526.46	108053.37	18473.54	2515.19
186	6	6	498.95	184.98	66341.48	108552.32	18658.52	3014.14
187	7	6	497.56	186.37	66155.11	109049.88	18844.89	3511.70
188	8	6	496.16	187.77	65967.35	109546.04	19032.65	4007.87
189	9	6	494.76	189.17	65778.17	110040.80	19221.83	4502.62
190	10	6	493.34	190.59	65587.58	110534.13	19412.42	4995.96
191	11	6	491.91	192.02	65395.56	111026.04	19604.44	5487.86
192	12	6	490.47	193.46	65202.09	111516.51	19797.91	5978.33
193	1	7	489.02	194.91	65007.18	112005.52	19992.82	489.02
194	2	7	487.55	196.38	64810.81	112493.08	20189.19	976.57
195	3	7	486.08	197.85	64612.96	112979.16	20387.04	1462.65
196	4	7	484.60	199.33	64413.63	113463.75	20586.37	1947.25
197	5	7	483.10	200.83	64212.80	113946.86	20787.20	2430.35
198	6	7	481.60	202.33	64010.47	114428.45	20989.53	2911.95
199	7	7	480.08	203.85	63806.61	114908.53	21193.39	3392.02
200	8	7	478.55	205.38	63601.23	115387.08	21398.77	3870.57
201	9	7	477.01	206.92	63394.31	115864.09	21605.69	4347.58
202	10	7	475.46	208.47	63185.84	116339.55	21814.16	4823.04
203	11	7	473.89	210.04	62975.81	116813.44	22024.19	5296.93
204	12	7	472.32	211.61	62764.20	117285.76	22235.80	5769.25
205	1	8	470.73	213.20	62551.00	117756.49	22449.00	470.73
206	2	8	469.13	214.80	62336.20	118225.62	22663.80	939.86
207	3	8	467.52	216.41	62119.79	118693.14	22880.21	1407.39
208	4	8	465.90	218.03	61901.76	119159.04	23098.24	1873.28
209	5	8	464.26	219.67	61682.10	119623.31	23317.90	2337.55
210	6	8	462.62	221.31	61460.78	120085.92	23539.22	2800.16

Payment			For this Month			Cumulative		
No.	Mo.	Yr.	Interest	Principal	Balance	Interest	Principal	Int. for Yr.
211	7	8	460.96	222.97	61237.81	120546.88	23762.19	3261.12
212	8	8	459.28	224.65	61013.17	121006.16	23986.83	3720.40
213	9	8	457.60	226.33	60786.84	121463.76	24213.16	4178.00
214	10	8	455.90	228.03	60558.81	121919.66	24441.19	4633.90
215	11	8	454.19	229.74	60329.07	122373.85	24670.93	5088.09
216	12	8	452.47	231.46	60097.61	122826.32	24902.39	5540.56
217	1	9	450.73	233.20	59864.41	123277.05	25135.59	450.73
218	2	9	448.98	234.95	59629.46	123726.04	25370.54	899.72
219	3	9	447.22	236.71	59392.76	124173.26	25607.24	1346.94
220	4	9	445.45	238.48	59154.27	124618.70	25845.73	1792.38
221	5	9	443.66	240.27	58914.00	125062.36	26086.00	2236.04
222	6	9	441.86	242.07	58671.93	125504.21	26328.07	2677.89
223	7	9	440.04	243.89	58428.04	125944.25	26571.96	3117.93
224	8	9	438.21	245.72	58182.32	126382.46	26817.68	3556.14
225	9	9	436.37	247.56	57934.76	126818.83	27065.24	3992.51
226	10	9	434.51	249.42	57685.34	127253.34	27314.66	4427.02
227	11	9	432.64	251.29	57434.05	127685.98	27565.95	4859.66
228	12	9	430.76	253.17	57180.87	128116.74	27819.13	5290.42
229	1	10	428.86	255.07	56925.80	128545.59	28074.20	428.86
230	2	10	426.94	256.99	56668.82	128972.54	28331.18	855.80
231	3	10	425.02	258.91	56409.90	129397.55	28590.10	1280.82
232	4	10	423.07	260.85	56149.05	129820.63	28850.95	1703.89
233	5	10	421.12	262.81	55886.24	130241.75	29113.76	2125.01
234	6	10	419.15	264.78	55621.45	130660.89	29378.55	2544.16
235	7	10	417.16	266.77	55354.69	131078.05	29645.31	2961.32
236	8	10	415.16	268.77	55085.92	131493.21	29914.08	3376.48
237	9	10	413.14	270.78	54815.13	131906.36	30184.87	3789.62
238	10	10	411.11	272.82	54542.32	132317.47	30457.68	4200.73
239	11	10	409.07	274.86	54267.45	132726.54	30732.55	4609.80
240	12	10	407.01	276.92	53990.53	133133.54	31009.47	5016.81
241	1	11	404.93	279.00	53711.53	133538.47	31288.47	404.93
242	2	11	402.84	281.09	53430.44	133941.31	31569.56	807.77
243	3	11	400.73	283.20	53147.24	134342.04	31852.76	1208.49
244	4	11	398.60	285.32	52861.91	134740.64	32138.09	1607.10
245	5	11	396.46	287.46	52574.45	135137.11	32425.55	2003.56
246	6	11	394.31	289.62	52284.83	135531.42	32715.17	2397.87
247	7	11	392.14	291.79	51993.03	135923.55	33006.97	2790.01
248	8	11	389.95	293.98	51699.05	136313.50	33300.95	3179.95
249	9	11	387.74	296.19	51402.87	136701.24	33597.13	3567.70
250	10	11	385.52	298.41	51104.46	137086.76	33895.54	3953.22
251	11	11	383.28	300.65	50803.81	137470.05	34196.19	4336.50
252	12	11	381.03	302.90	50500.91	137851.08	34499.09	4717.53
253	1	12	378.76	305.17	50195.74	138229.83	34804.26	378.76
254	2	12	376.47	307.46	49888.28	138606.30	35111.72	755.22
255	3	12	374.16	309.77	49578.51	138980.46	35421.49	1129.39
256	4	12	371.84	312.09	49266.42	139352.30	35733.58	1501.23

Payment			For this Month			Cumulative		
No.	Mo.	Yr.	Interest	Principal	Balance	Interest	Principal	Int. for Yr.
257	5	12	369.50	314.43	48951.99	139721.80	36048.01	1870.72
258	6	12	367.14	316.79	48635.20	140088.94	36364.80	2237.86
259	7	12	364.76	319.17	48316.03	140453.70	36683.97	2602.63
260	8	12	362.37	321.56	47994.48	140816.07	37005.52	2965.00
261	9	12	359.96	323.97	47670.50	141176.03	37329.50	3324.96
262	10	12	357.53	326.40	47344.10	141533.56	37655.90	3682.49
263	11	12	355.08	328.85	47015.26	141888.64	37984.74	4037.57
264	12	12	352.61	331.31	46683.94	142241.26	38316.06	4390.18
265	1	13	350.13	333.80	46350.14	142591.39	38649.86	350.13
266	2	13	347.63	336.30	46013.84	142939.01	38986.16	697.76
267	3	13	345.10	338.83	45675.01	143284.12	39324.99	1042.86
268	4	13	342.56	341.37	45333.65	143626.68	39666.35	1385.42
269	5	13	340.00	343.93	44989.72	143966.68	40010.28	1725.42
270	6	13	337.42	346.51	44643.21	144304.10	40356.79	2062.85
271	7	13	334.82	349.11	44294.11	144638.93	40705.89	2397.67
272	8	13	332.21	351.72	43942.38	144971.13	41057.62	2729.88
273	9	13	329.57	354.36	43588.02	145300.70	41411.98	3059.45
274	10	13	326.91	357.02	43231.00	145627.61	41769.00	3386.36
275	11	13	324.23	359.70	42871.31	145951.84	42128.69	3710.59
276	12	13	321.53	362.39	42508.91	146273.38	42491.09	4032.12
277	1	14	318.82	365.11	42143.80	146592.20	42856.20	318.82
278	2	14	316.08	367.85	41775.95	146908.27	43224.05	634.90
279	3	14	313.32	370.61	41405.34	147221.59	43594.66	948.21
280	4	14	310.54	373.39	41031.95	147532.13	43968.05	1258.76
281	5	14	307.74	376.19	40655.76	147839.87	44344.24	1566.49
282	6	14	304.92	379.01	40276.75	148144.79	44723.25	1871.41
283	7	14	302.08	381.85	39894.90	148446.87	45105.10	2173.49
284	8	14	299.21	384.72	39510.18	148746.08	45489.82	2472.70
285	9	14	296.33	387.60	39122.58	149042.41	45877.42	2769.03
286	10	14	293.42	390.51	38732.07	149335.82	46267.93	3062.45
287	11	14	290.49	393.44	38338.63	149626.32	46661.37	3352.94
288	12	14	287.54	396.39	37942.24	149913.85	47057.76	3640.48
289	1	15	284.57	399.36	37542.88	150198.42	47457.12	284.57
290	2	15	281.57	402.36	37140.52	150479.99	47859.48	566.14
291	3	15	278.55	405.38	36735.14	150758.55	48264.86	844.69
292	4	15	275.51	408.42	36326.73	151034.06	48673.27	1120.21
293	5	15	272.45	411.48	35915.25	151306.51	49084.75	1392.66
294	6	15	269.36	414.56	35500.68	151575.88	49499.32	1662.02
295	7	15	266.26	417.67	35083.01	151842.13	49916.99	1928.28
296	8	15	263.12	420.81	34662.20	152105.25	50337.80	2191.40
297	9	15	259.97	423.96	34238.24	152365.22	50761.76	2451.36
298	10	15	256.79	427.14	33811.10	152622.01	51188.90	2708.15
299	11	15	253.58	430.35	33380.75	152875.59	51619.25	2961.73
300	12	15	250.36	433.57	32947.18	153125.95	52052.82	3212.09
301	1	16	247.10	436.83	32510.35	153373.05	52489.65	247.10
302	2	16	243.83	440.10	32070.25	153616.88	52929.75	490.93

Payment			For this Month			Cumulative		
No.	Mo.	Yr.	Interest	Principal	Balance	Interest	Principal	Int. for Yr.
303	3	16	240.53	443.40	31626.85	153857.40	53373.15	731.46
304	4	16	237.20	446.73	31180.12	154094.61	53819.88	968.66
305	5	16	233.85	450.08	30730.04	154328.46	54269.96	1202.51
306	6	16	230.48	453.45	30276.59	154558.93	54723.41	1432.99
307	7	16	227.07	456.85	29819.73	154786.01	55180.27	1660.06
308	8	16	223.65	460.28	29359.45	155009.65	55640.55	1883.71
309	9	16	220.20	463.73	28895.72	155229.85	56104.28	2103.90
310	10	16	216.72	467.21	28428.51	155446.57	56571.49	2320.62
311	11	16	213.21	470.72	27957.79	155659.78	57042.21	2533.84
312	12	16	209.68	474.25	27483.55	155869.46	57516.45	2743.52
313	1	17	206.13	477.80	27005.74	156075.59	57994.26	206.13
314	2	17	202.54	481.39	26524.36	156278.13	58475.64	408.67
315	3	17	198.93	485.00	26039.36	156477.07	58960.64	607.60
316	4	17	195.30	488.63	25550.73	156672.36	59449.27	802.90
317	5	17	191.63	492.30	25058.43	156863.99	59941.57	994.53
318	6	17	187.94	495.99	24562.44	157051.93	60437.56	1182.47
319	7	17	184.22	499.71	24062.73	157236.15	60937.27	1366.68
320	8	17	180.47	503.46	23559.27	157416.62	61440.73	1547.15
321	9	17	176.69	507.23	23052.03	157593.31	61947.97	1723.85
322	10	17	172.89	511.04	22540.99	157766.20	62459.01	1896.74
323	11	17	169.06	514.87	22026.12	157935.26	62973.88	2065.80
324	12	17	165.20	518.73	21507.39	158100.46	63492.61	2230.99
325	1	18	161.31	522.62	20984.77	158261.76	64015.23	161.31
326	2	18	157.39	526.54	20458.22	158419.15	64541.78	318.69
327	3	18	153.44	530.49	19927.73	158572.59	65072.27	472.13
328	4	18	149.46	534.47	19393.26	158722.04	65606.74	621.59
329	5	18	145.45	538.48	18854.78	158867.49	66145.22	767.04
330	6	18	141.41	542.52	18312.26	159008.90	66687.74	908.45
331	7	18	137.34	546.59	17765.67	159146.25	67234.33	1045.79
332	8	18	133.24	550.69	17214.99	159279.49	67785.01	1179.03
333	9	18	129.11	554.82	16660.17	159408.60	68339.83	1308.14
334	10	18	124.95	558.98	16101.19	159533.55	68898.81	1433.09
335	11	18	120.76	563.17	15538.02	159654.31	69461.98	1553.85
336	12	18	116.54	567.39	14970.63	159770.85	70029.37	1670.39
337	1	19	112.28	571.65	14398.98	159883.13	70601.02	112.28
338	2	19	107.99	575.94	13823.04	159991.12	71176.96	220.27
339	3	19	103.67	580.26	13242.78	160094.79	71757.22	323.94
340	4	19	99.32	584.61	12658.18	160194.11	72341.82	423.27
341	5	19	94.94	588.99	12069.18	160289.05	72930.82	518.20
342	6	19	90.52	593.41	11475.77	160379.57	73524.23	608.72
343	7	19	86.07	597.86	10877.91	160465.64	74122.09	694.79
344	8	19	81.58	602.34	10275.57	160547.22	74724.43	776.37
345	9	19	77.07	606.86	9668.70	160624.29	75331.30	853.44
346	10	19	72.52	611.41	9057.29	160696.80	75942.71	925.96
347	11	19	67.93	616.00	8441.29	160764.73	76558.71	993.89
348	12	19	63.31	620.62	7820.67	160828.04	77179.33	1057.19

Payment			For this Month			Cumulative		
No.	Mo.	Yr.	Interest	Principal	Balance	Interest	Principal	Int. for Yr.
349	1	20	58.66	625.27	7195.40	160886.70	77804.60	58.66
350	2	20	53.97	629.96	6565.43	160940.66	78434.57	112.62
351	3	20	49.24	634.69	5930.74	160989.90	79069.26	161.86
352	4	20	44.48	639.45	5291.30	161034.38	79708.70	206.34
353	5	20	39.68	644.24	4647.05	161074.07	80352.95	246.03
354	6	20	34.85	649.08	3997.98	161108.92	81002.02	280.88
355	7	20	29.98	653.94	3344.03	161138.91	81655.97	310.86
356	8	20	25.08	658.85	2685.18	161163.99	82314.82	335.94
357	9	20	20.14	663.79	2021.39	161184.12	82978.61	356.08
358	10	20	15.16	668.77	1352.62	161199.28	83647.38	371.24
359	11	20	10.14	673.78	678.84	161209.43	84321.16	381.39
360	12	20	5.09	678.84	0.00	161214.52	85000.00	386.48

Loan Account Information

Name:	Gary Sanseri
Address:	8431 S.E. 36th Ave.
City, State ZIP:	Portland, OR 97222
Telephone:	505-654-2300
Reference:	Loan No. 50637

Loan Data

Original Loan Amount:	85000.00
Original Loan Date (mo.yr):	1.91
Annual Interest Rate:	9.00
Original Loan Period - Months:	360
User Entered Monthly Payment:	
Calculated Monthly Loan Payment:	683.93
Total Calculated Payments:	246214.80
Total Calculated Interest:	161214.80

sample loan with $25 prepayment

Pmt No.	Payment Mo	Yr	Interest Portion	Principal Portion	Additional Principal	Remaining Loan Balance	Interest for Year	Cumulative Interest
1	2	91	637.50	46.43	25.00	84928.57	637.50	637.5
2	3	91	636.96	46.97	25.00	84856.60	1274.46	1274.46
3	4	91	636.42	47.51	25.00	84784.09	1910.88	1910.88
4	5	91	635.88	48.05	25.00	84711.04	2546.76	2546.76
5	6	91	635.33	48.60	25.00	84637.44	3182.09	3182.09
6	7	91	634.78	49.15	25.00	84563.29	3816.87	3816.87
7	8	91	634.22	49.71	25.00	84488.58	4451.09	4451.09
8	9	91	633.66	50.27	25.00	84413.31	5084.75	5084.75
9	10	91	633.10	50.83	25.00	84337.48	5717.85	5717.85
10	11	91	632.53	51.40	25.00	84261.08	6350.38	6350.38
11	12	91	631.96	51.97	25.00	84184.11	6982.34	6982.34
12	1	92	631.38	52.55	25.00	84106.56	631.38	7613.72
13	2	92	630.80	53.13	25.00	84028.43	1262.18	8244.52
14	3	92	630.21	53.72	25.00	83949.71	1892.39	8874.73
15	4	92	629.62	54.31	25.00	83870.40	2522.01	9504.35
16	5	92	629.03	54.90	25.00	83790.50	3151.04	10133.38
17	6	92	628.43	55.50	25.00	83710.00	3779.47	10761.81
18	7	92	627.83	56.10	25.00	83628.90	4407.30	11389.64
19	8	92	627.22	56.71	25.00	83547.19	5034.52	12016.86
20	9	92	626.60	57.33	25.00	83464.86	5661.12	12643.46
21	10	92	625.99	57.94	25.00	83381.92	6287.11	13269.45
22	11	92	625.36	58.57	25.00	83298.35	6912.47	13894.81
23	12	92	624.74	59.19	25.00	83214.16	7537.21	14519.55
24	1	93	624.11	59.82	25.00	83129.34	624.11	15143.66
25	2	93	623.47	60.46	25.00	83043.88	1247.58	15767.13
26	3	93	622.83	61.10	25.00	82957.78	1870.41	16389.96
27	4	93	622.18	61.75	25.00	82871.03	2492.59	17012.14
28	5	93	621.53	62.40	25.00	82783.63	3114.12	17633.67
29	6	93	620.88	63.05	25.00	82695.58	3735.00	18254.55

Pmt No.	Payment Mo	Payment Yr	Interest Portion	Principal Portion	Additional Principal	Remaining Loan Balance	Interest for Year	Cumulative Interest
30	7	93	620.22	63.71	25.00	82606.87	4355.22	18874.77
31	8	93	619.55	64.38	25.00	82517.49	4974.77	19494.32
32	9	93	618.88	65.05	25.00	82427.44	5593.65	20113.20
33	10	93	618.21	65.72	25.00	82336.72	6211.86	20731.41
34	11	93	617.53	66.40	25.00	82245.32	6829.39	21348.94
35	12	93	616.84	67.09	25.00	82153.23	7446.23	21965.78
36	1	94	616.15	67.78	25.00	82060.45	616.15	22581.93
37	2	94	615.45	68.48	25.00	81966.97	1231.60	23197.38
38	3	94	614.75	69.18	25.00	81872.79	1846.35	23812.13
39	4	94	614.05	69.88	25.00	81777.91	2460.40	24426.18
40	5	94	613.33	70.60	25.00	81682.31	3073.73	25039.51
41	6	94	612.62	71.31	25.00	81586.00	3686.35	25652.13
42	7	94	611.90	72.03	25.00	81488.97	4298.25	26264.03
43	8	94	611.17	72.76	25.00	81391.21	4909.42	26875.20
44	9	94	610.43	73.50	25.00	81292.71	5519.85	27485.63
45	10	94	609.70	74.23	25.00	81193.48	6129.55	28095.33
46	11	94	608.95	74.98	25.00	81093.50	6738.50	28704.28
47	12	94	608.20	75.73	25.00	80992.77	7346.70	29312.48
48	1	95	607.45	76.48	25.00	80891.29	607.45	29919.93
49	2	95	606.68	77.25	25.00	80789.04	1214.13	30526.61
50	3	95	605.92	78.01	25.00	80686.03	1820.05	31132.53
51	4	95	605.15	78.78	25.00	80582.25	2425.20	31737.68
52	5	95	604.37	79.56	25.00	80477.69	3029.57	32342.05
53	6	95	603.58	80.35	25.00	80372.34	3633.15	32945.63
54	7	95	602.79	81.14	25.00	80266.20	4235.94	33548.42
55	8	95	602.00	81.93	25.00	80159.27	4837.94	34150.42
56	9	95	601.19	82.74	25.00	80051.53	5439.13	34751.61
57	10	95	600.39	83.54	25.00	79942.99	6039.52	35352.00
58	11	95	599.57	84.36	25.00	79833.63	6639.09	35951.57
59	12	95	598.75	85.18	25.00	79723.45	7237.84	36550.32
60	1	96	597.93	86.00	25.00	79612.45	597.93	37148.25
61	2	96	597.09	86.84	25.00	79500.61	1195.02	37745.34
62	3	96	596.25	87.68	25.00	79387.93	1791.27	38341.59
63	4	96	595.41	88.52	25.00	79274.41	2386.68	38937.00
64	5	96	594.56	89.37	25.00	79160.04	2981.24	39531.56
65	6	96	593.70	90.23	25.00	79044.81	3574.94	40125.26
66	7	96	592.84	91.09	25.00	78928.72	4167.78	40718.10
67	8	96	591.97	91.96	25.00	78811.76	4759.75	41310.07
68	9	96	591.09	92.84	25.00	78693.92	5350.84	41901.16
69	10	96	590.20	93.73	25.00	78575.19	5941.04	42491.36
70	11	96	589.31	94.62	25.00	78455.57	6530.35	43080.67
71	12	96	588.42	95.51	25.00	78335.06	7118.77	43669.09
72	1	97	587.51	96.42	25.00	78213.64	587.51	44256.60
73	2	97	586.60	97.33	25.00	78091.31	1174.11	44843.20
74	3	97	585.68	98.25	25.00	77968.06	1759.79	45428.88
75	4	97	584.76	99.17	25.00	77843.89	2344.55	46013.64

Pmt No.	Payment Mo	Yr	Interest Portion	Principal Portion	Additional Principal	Remaining Loan Balance	Interest for Year	Cumulative Interest
76	5	97	583.83	100.10	25.00	77718.79	2928.38	46597.47
77	6	97	582.89	101.04	25.00	77592.75	3511.27	47180.36
78	7	97	581.95	101.98	25.00	77465.77	4093.22	47762.31
79	8	97	580.99	102.94	25.00	77337.83	4674.21	48343.30
80	9	97	580.03	103.90	25.00	77208.93	5254.24	48923.33
81	10	97	579.07	104.86	25.00	77079.07	5833.31	49502.40
82	11	97	578.09	105.84	25.00	76948.23	6411.40	50080.49
83	12	97	577.11	106.82	25.00	76816.41	6988.51	50657.60
84	1	98	576.12	107.81	25.00	76683.60	576.12	51233.72
85	2	98	575.13	108.80	25.00	76549.80	1151.25	51808.85
86	3	98	574.12	109.81	25.00	76414.99	1725.37	52382.97
87	4	98	573.11	110.82	25.00	76279.17	2298.48	52956.08
88	5	98	572.09	111.84	25.00	76142.33	2870.57	53528.17
89	6	98	571.07	112.86	25.00	76004.47	3441.64	54099.24
90	7	98	570.03	113.90	25.00	75865.57	4011.67	54669.27
91	8	98	568.99	114.94	25.00	75725.63	4580.66	55238.26
92	9	98	567.94	115.99	25.00	75584.64	5148.60	55806.20
93	10	98	566.88	117.05	25.00	75442.59	5715.48	56373.08
94	11	98	565.82	118.11	25.00	75299.48	6281.30	56938.90
95	12	98	564.75	119.18	25.00	75155.30	6846.05	57503.65
96	1	99	563.66	120.27	25.00	75010.03	563.66	58067.31
97	2	99	562.58	121.35	25.00	74863.68	1126.24	58629.89
98	3	99	561.48	122.45	25.00	74716.23	1687.72	59191.37
99	4	99	560.37	123.56	25.00	74567.67	2248.09	59751.74
100	5	99	559.26	124.67	25.00	74418.00	2807.35	60311.00
101	6	99	558.14	125.79	25.00	74267.21	3365.49	60869.14
102	7	99	557.00	126.93	25.00	74115.28	3922.49	61426.14
103	8	99	555.86	128.07	25.00	73962.21	4478.35	61982.00
104	9	99	554.72	129.21	25.00	73808.00	5033.07	62536.72
105	10	99	553.56	130.37	25.00	73652.63	5586.63	63090.28
106	11	99	552.39	131.54	25.00	73496.09	6139.02	63642.67
107	12	99	551.22	132.71	25.00	73338.38	6690.24	64193.89
108	1	0	550.04	133.89	25.00	73179.49	550.04	64743.93
109	2	0	548.85	135.08	25.00	73019.41	1098.89	65292.78
110	3	0	547.65	136.28	25.00	72858.13	1646.54	65840.43
111	4	0	546.44	137.49	25.00	72695.64	2192.98	66386.87
112	5	0	545.22	138.71	25.00	72531.93	2738.20	66932.09
113	6	0	543.99	139.94	25.00	72366.99	3282.19	67476.08
114	7	0	542.75	141.18	25.00	72200.81	3824.94	68018.83
115	8	0	541.51	142.42	25.00	72033.39	4366.45	68560.34
116	9	0	540.25	143.68	25.00	71864.71	4906.70	69100.59
117	10	0	538.99	144.94	25.00	71694.77	5445.69	69639.58
118	11	0	537.71	146.22	25.00	71523.55	5983.40	70177.29
119	12	0	536.43	147.50	25.00	71351.05	6519.83	70713.72
120	1	1	535.13	148.80	25.00	71177.25	535.13	71248.85
121	2	1	533.83	150.10	25.00	71002.15	1068.96	71782.68

Pmt No.	Mo	Yr	Interest Portion	Principal Portion	Additional Principal	Remaining Loan Balance	Interest for Year	Cumulative Interest
122	3	1	532.52	151.41	25.00	70825.74	1601.48	72315.20
123	4	1	531.19	152.74	25.00	70648.00	2132.67	72846.39
124	5	1	529.86	154.07	25.00	70468.93	2662.53	73376.25
125	6	1	528.52	155.41	25.00	70288.52	3191.05	73904.77
126	7	1	527.16	156.77	25.00	70106.75	3718.21	74431.93
127	8	1	525.80	158.13	25.00	69923.62	4244.01	74957.73
128	9	1	524.43	159.50	25.00	69739.12	4768.44	75482.16
129	10	1	523.04	160.89	25.00	69553.23	5291.48	76005.20
130	11	1	521.65	162.28	25.00	69365.95	5813.13	76526.85
131	12	1	520.24	163.69	25.00	69177.26	6333.37	77047.09
132	1	2	518.83	165.10	25.00	68987.16	518.83	77565.92
133	2	2	517.40	166.53	25.00	68795.63	1036.23	78083.32
134	3	2	515.97	167.96	25.00	68602.67	1552.20	78599.29
135	4	2	514.52	169.41	25.00	68408.26	2066.72	79113.81
136	5	2	513.06	170.87	25.00	68212.39	2579.78	79626.87
137	6	2	511.59	172.34	25.00	68015.05	3091.37	80138.46
138	7	2	510.11	173.82	25.00	67816.23	3601.48	80648.57
139	8	2	508.62	175.31	25.00	67615.92	4110.10	81157.19
140	9	2	507.12	176.81	25.00	67414.11	4617.22	81664.31
141	10	2	505.61	178.32	25.00	67210.79	5122.83	82169.92
142	11	2	504.08	179.85	25.00	67005.94	5626.91	82674.00
143	12	2	502.54	181.39	25.00	66799.55	6129.45	83176.54
144	1	3	501.00	182.93	25.00	66591.62	501.00	83677.54
145	2	3	499.44	184.49	25.00	66382.13	1000.44	84176.98
146	3	3	497.87	186.06	25.00	66171.07	1498.31	84674.85
147	4	3	496.28	187.65	25.00	65958.42	1994.59	85171.13
148	5	3	494.69	189.24	25.00	65744.18	2489.28	85665.82
149	6	3	493.08	190.85	25.00	65528.33	2982.36	86158.90
150	7	3	491.46	192.47	25.00	65310.86	3473.82	86650.36
151	8	3	489.83	194.10	25.00	65091.76	3963.65	87140.19
152	9	3	488.19	195.74	25.00	64871.02	4451.84	87628.38
153	10	3	486.53	197.40	25.00	64648.62	4938.37	88114.91
154	11	3	484.86	199.07	25.00	64424.55	5423.23	88599.77
155	12	3	483.18	200.75	25.00	64198.80	5906.41	89082.95
156	1	4	481.49	202.44	25.00	63971.36	481.49	89564.44
157	2	4	479.79	204.14	25.00	63742.22	961.28	90044.23
158	3	4	478.07	205.86	25.00	63511.36	1439.35	90522.30
159	4	4	476.34	207.59	25.00	63278.77	1915.69	90998.64
160	5	4	474.59	209.34	25.00	63044.43	2390.28	91473.23
161	6	4	472.83	211.10	25.00	62808.33	2863.11	91946.06
162	7	4	471.06	212.87	25.00	62570.46	3334.17	92417.12
163	8	4	469.28	214.65	25.00	62330.81	3803.45	92886.40
164	9	4	467.48	216.45	25.00	62089.36	4270.93	93353.88
165	10	4	465.67	218.26	25.00	61846.10	4736.60	93819.55
166	11	4	463.85	220.08	25.00	61601.02	5200.45	94283.40
167	12	4	462.01	221.92	25.00	61354.10	5662.46	94745.41

Pmt No.	Payment Mo	Yr	Interest Portion	Principal Portion	Additional Principal	Remaining Loan Balance	Interest for Year	Cumulative Interest
168	1	5	460.16	223.77	25.00	61105.33	460.16	95205.57
169	2	5	458.29	225.64	25.00	60854.69	918.45	95663.86
170	3	5	456.41	227.52	25.00	60602.17	1374.86	96120.27
171	4	5	454.52	229.41	25.00	60347.76	1829.38	96574.79
172	5	5	452.61	231.32	25.00	60091.44	2281.99	97027.40
173	6	5	450.69	233.24	25.00	59833.20	2732.68	97478.09
174	7	5	448.75	235.18	25.00	59573.02	3181.43	97926.84
175	8	5	446.80	237.13	25.00	59310.89	3628.23	98373.64
176	9	5	444.83	239.10	25.00	59046.79	4073.06	98818.47
177	10	5	442.85	241.08	25.00	58780.71	4515.91	99261.32
178	11	5	440.86	243.07	25.00	58512.64	4956.77	99702.18
179	12	5	438.84	245.09	25.00	58242.55	5395.61	100141.02
180	1	6	436.82	247.11	25.00	57970.44	436.82	100577.84
181	2	6	434.78	249.15	25.00	57696.29	871.60	101012.62
182	3	6	432.72	251.21	25.00	57420.08	1304.32	101445.34
183	4	6	430.65	253.28	25.00	57141.80	1734.97	101875.99
184	5	6	428.56	255.37	25.00	56861.43	2163.53	102304.55
185	6	6	426.46	257.47	25.00	56578.96	2589.99	102731.01
186	7	6	424.34	259.59	25.00	56294.37	3014.33	103155.35
187	8	6	422.21	261.72	25.00	56007.65	3436.54	103577.56
188	9	6	420.06	263.87	25.00	55718.78	3856.60	103997.62
189	10	6	417.89	266.04	25.00	55427.74	4274.49	104415.51
190	11	6	415.71	268.22	25.00	55134.52	4690.20	104831.22
191	12	6	413.51	270.42	25.00	54839.10	5103.71	105244.73
192	1	7	411.29	272.64	25.00	54541.46	411.29	105656.02
193	2	7	409.06	274.87	25.00	54241.59	820.35	106065.08
194	3	7	406.81	277.12	25.00	53939.47	1227.16	106471.89
195	4	7	404.55	279.38	25.00	53635.09	1631.71	106876.44
196	5	7	402.26	281.67	25.00	53328.42	2033.97	107278.70
197	6	7	399.96	283.97	25.00	53019.45	2433.93	107678.66
198	7	7	397.65	286.28	25.00	52708.17	2831.58	108076.31
199	8	7	395.31	288.62	25.00	52394.55	3226.89	108471.62
200	9	7	392.96	290.97	25.00	52078.58	3619.85	108864.58
201	10	7	390.59	293.34	25.00	51760.24	4010.44	109255.17
202	11	7	388.20	295.73	25.00	51439.51	4398.64	109643.37
203	12	7	385.80	298.13	25.00	51116.38	4784.44	110029.17
204	1	8	383.37	300.56	25.00	50790.82	383.37	110412.54
205	2	8	380.93	303.00	25.00	50462.82	764.30	110793.47
206	3	8	378.47	305.46	25.00	50132.36	1142.77	111171.94
207	4	8	375.99	307.94	25.00	49799.42	1518.76	111547.93
208	5	8	373.50	310.43	25.00	49463.99	1892.26	111921.43
209	6	8	370.98	312.95	25.00	49126.04	2263.24	112292.41
210	7	8	368.45	315.48	25.00	48785.56	2631.69	112660.86
211	8	8	365.89	318.04	25.00	48442.52	2997.58	113026.75
212	9	8	363.32	320.61	25.00	48096.91	3360.90	113390.07
213	10	8	360.73	323.20	25.00	47748.71	3721.63	113750.80

Pmt No.	Payment Mo	Yr	Interest Portion	Principal Portion	Additional Principal	Remaining Loan Balance	Interest for Year	Cumulative Interest
214	11	8	358.12	325.81	25.00	47397.90	4079.75	114108.92
215	12	8	355.48	328.45	25.00	47044.45	4435.23	114464.40
216	1	9	352.83	331.10	25.00	46688.35	352.83	114817.23
217	2	9	350.16	333.77	25.00	46329.58	702.99	115167.39
218	3	9	347.47	336.46	25.00	45968.12	1050.46	115514.86
219	4	9	344.76	339.17	25.00	45603.95	1395.22	115859.62
220	5	9	342.03	341.90	25.00	45237.05	1737.25	116201.65
221	6	9	339.28	344.65	25.00	44867.40	2076.53	116540.93
222	7	9	336.51	347.42	25.00	44494.98	2413.04	116877.44
223	8	9	333.71	350.22	25.00	44119.76	2746.75	117211.15
224	9	9	330.90	353.03	25.00	43741.73	3077.65	117542.05
225	10	9	328.06	355.87	25.00	43360.86	3405.71	117870.11
226	11	9	325.21	358.72	25.00	42977.14	3730.92	118195.32
227	12	9	322.33	361.60	25.00	42590.54	4053.25	118517.65
228	1	10	319.43	364.50	25.00	42201.04	319.43	118837.08
229	2	10	316.51	367.42	25.00	41808.62	635.94	119153.59
230	3	10	313.56	370.37	25.00	41413.25	949.50	119467.15
231	4	10	310.60	373.33	25.00	41014.92	1260.10	119777.75
232	5	10	307.61	376.32	25.00	40613.60	1567.71	120085.36
233	6	10	304.60	379.33	25.00	40209.27	1872.31	120389.96
234	7	10	301.57	382.36	25.00	39801.91	2173.88	120691.53
235	8	10	298.51	385.42	25.00	39391.49	2472.39	120990.04
236	9	10	295.44	388.49	25.00	38978.00	2767.83	121285.48
237	10	10	292.33	391.60	25.00	38561.40	3060.16	121577.81
238	11	10	289.21	394.72	25.00	38141.68	3349.37	121867.02
239	12	10	286.06	397.87	25.00	37718.81	3635.43	122153.08
240	1	11	282.89	401.04	25.00	37292.77	282.89	122435.97
241	2	11	279.70	404.23	25.00	36863.54	562.59	122715.67
242	3	11	276.48	407.45	25.00	36431.09	839.07	122992.15
243	4	11	273.23	410.70	25.00	35995.39	1112.30	123265.38
244	5	11	269.97	413.96	25.00	35556.43	1382.27	123535.35
245	6	11	266.67	417.26	25.00	35114.17	1648.94	123802.02
246	7	11	263.36	420.57	25.00	34668.60	1912.30	124065.38
247	8	11	260.01	423.92	25.00	34219.68	2172.31	124325.39
248	9	11	256.65	427.28	25.00	33767.40	2428.96	124582.04
249	10	11	253.26	430.67	25.00	33311.73	2682.22	124835.30
250	11	11	249.84	434.09	25.00	32852.64	2932.06	125085.14
251	12	11	246.39	437.54	25.00	32390.10	3178.45	125331.53
252	1	12	242.93	441.00	25.00	31924.10	242.93	125574.46
253	2	12	239.43	444.50	25.00	31454.60	482.36	125813.89
254	3	12	235.91	448.02	25.00	30981.58	718.27	126049.80
255	4	12	232.36	451.57	25.00	30505.01	950.63	126282.16
256	5	12	228.79	455.14	25.00	30024.87	1179.42	126510.95
257	6	12	225.19	458.74	25.00	29541.13	1404.61	126736.14
258	7	12	221.56	462.37	25.00	29053.76	1626.17	126957.70
259	8	12	217.90	466.03	25.00	28562.73	1844.07	127175.60

Pmt No.	Payment Mo	Yr	Interest Portion	Principal Portion	Additional Principal	Remaining Loan Balance	Interest for Year	Cumulative Interest
260	9	12	214.22	469.71	25.00	28068.02	2058.29	127389.82
261	10	12	210.51	473.42	25.00	27569.60	2268.80	127600.33
262	11	12	206.77	477.16	25.00	27067.44	2475.57	127807.10
263	12	12	203.01	480.92	25.00	26561.52	2678.58	128010.11
264	1	13	199.21	484.72	25.00	26051.80	199.21	128209.32
265	2	13	195.39	488.54	25.00	25538.26	394.60	128404.71
266	3	13	191.54	492.39	25.00	25020.87	586.14	128596.25
267	4	13	187.66	496.27	25.00	24499.60	773.80	128783.91
268	5	13	183.75	500.18	25.00	23974.42	957.55	128967.66
269	6	13	179.81	504.12	25.00	23445.30	1137.36	129147.47
270	7	13	175.84	508.09	25.00	22912.21	1313.20	129323.31
271	8	13	171.84	512.09	25.00	22375.12	1485.04	129495.15
272	9	13	167.81	516.12	25.00	21834.00	1652.85	129662.96
273	10	13	163.75	520.18	25.00	21288.82	1816.60	129826.71
274	11	13	159.67	524.26	25.00	20739.56	1976.27	129986.38
275	12	13	155.55	528.38	25.00	20186.18	2131.82	130141.93
276	1	14	151.40	532.53	25.00	19628.65	151.40	130293.33
277	2	14	147.21	536.72	25.00	19066.93	298.61	130440.54
278	3	14	143.00	540.93	25.00	18501.00	441.61	130583.54
279	4	14	138.76	545.17	25.00	17930.83	580.37	130722.30
280	5	14	134.48	549.45	25.00	17356.38	714.85	130856.78
281	6	14	130.17	553.76	25.00	16777.62	845.02	130986.95
282	7	14	125.83	558.10	25.00	16194.52	970.85	131112.78
283	8	14	121.46	562.47	25.00	15607.05	1092.31	131234.24
284	9	14	117.05	566.88	25.00	15015.17	1209.36	131351.29
285	10	14	112.61	571.32	25.00	14418.85	1321.97	131463.90
286	11	14	108.14	575.79	25.00	13818.06	1430.11	131572.04
287	12	14	103.64	580.29	25.00	13212.77	1533.75	131675.68
288	1	15	99.10	584.83	25.00	12602.94	99.10	131774.78
289	2	15	94.52	589.41	25.00	11988.53	193.62	131869.30
290	3	15	89.91	594.02	25.00	11369.51	283.53	131959.21
291	4	15	85.27	598.66	25.00	10745.85	368.80	132044.48
292	5	15	80.59	603.34	25.00	10117.51	449.39	132125.07
293	6	15	75.88	608.05	25.00	9484.46	525.27	132200.95
294	7	15	71.13	612.80	25.00	8846.66	596.40	132272.08
295	8	15	66.35	617.58	25.00	8204.08	662.75	132338.43
296	9	15	61.53	622.40	25.00	7556.68	724.28	132399.96
297	10	15	56.68	627.25	25.00	6904.43	780.96	132456.64
298	11	15	51.78	632.15	25.00	6247.28	832.74	132508.42
299	12	15	46.85	637.08	25.00	5585.20	879.59	132555.27
300	1	16	41.89	642.04	25.00	4918.16	41.89	132597.16
301	2	16	36.89	647.04	25.00	4246.12	78.78	132634.05
302	3	16	31.85	652.08	25.00	3569.04	110.63	132665.90
303	4	16	26.77	657.16	25.00	2886.88	137.40	132692.67
304	5	16	21.65	662.28	25.00	2199.60	159.05	132714.32
305	6	16	16.50	667.43	25.00	1507.17	175.55	132730.82

Pmt No.	Payment Mo	Payment Yr	Interest Portion	Principal Portion	Additional Principal	Remaining Loan Balance	Interest for Year	Cumulative Interest
306	7	16	11.30	672.63	25.00	809.54	186.85	132742.12
307	8	16	6.07	677.86	25.00	106.68	192.92	132748.19
308	9	16	0.80	106.68	0.00	0.00	193.72	132748.99

Loan Account Information

Name: Gary Sanseri
Address: 8431 S.E. 36th Ave.
City, State ZIP: Portland, OR 97222
Telephone: 505-654-2300
Reference: Loan No. 50637

Loan Data

Original Loan Amount:	85000.00
Original Loan Date (mo.yr):	1.91
Annual Interest Rate:	9.00
Original Loan Period - Months:	360
User Entered Monthly Payment:	
Calculated Monthly Loan Payment:	683.93
Total Calculated Payments:	246214.80
Total Calculated Interest:	161214.80

sample loan with $50 prepayment

Pmt No.	Payment Mo	Yr	Interest Portion	Principal Portion	Additional Principal	Remaining Loan Balance	Interest for Year	Cumulative Interest
1	2	91	637.50	46.43	50.00	84903.57	637.50	637.5
2	3	91	636.78	47.15	50.00	84806.42	1274.28	1274.28
3	4	91	636.05	47.88	50.00	84708.54	1910.33	1910.33
4	5	91	635.31	48.62	50.00	84609.92	2545.64	2545.64
5	6	91	634.57	49.36	50.00	84510.56	3180.21	3180.21
6	7	91	633.83	50.10	50.00	84410.46	3814.04	3814.04
7	8	91	633.08	50.85	50.00	84309.61	4447.12	4447.12
8	9	91	632.32	51.61	50.00	84208.00	5079.44	5079.44
9	10	91	631.56	52.37	50.00	84105.63	5711.00	5711.00
10	11	91	630.79	53.14	50.00	84002.49	6341.79	6341.79
11	12	91	630.02	53.91	50.00	83898.58	6971.81	6971.81
12	1	92	629.24	54.69	50.00	83793.89	629.24	7601.05
13	2	92	628.45	55.48	50.00	83688.41	1257.69	8229.50
14	3	92	627.66	56.27	50.00	83582.14	1885.35	8857.16
15	4	92	626.87	57.06	50.00	83475.08	2512.22	9484.03
16	5	92	626.06	57.87	50.00	83367.21	3138.28	10110.09
17	6	92	625.25	58.68	50.00	83258.53	3763.53	10735.34
18	7	92	624.44	59.49	50.00	83149.04	4387.97	11359.78
19	8	92	623.62	60.31	50.00	83038.73	5011.59	11983.40
20	9	92	622.79	61.14	50.00	82927.59	5634.38	12606.19
21	10	92	621.96	61.97	50.00	82815.62	6256.34	13228.15
22	11	92	621.12	62.81	50.00	82702.81	6877.46	13849.27
23	12	92	620.27	63.66	50.00	82589.15	7497.73	14469.54
24	1	93	619.42	64.51	50.00	82474.64	619.42	15088.96
25	2	93	618.56	65.37	50.00	82359.27	1237.98	15707.52
26	3	93	617.69	66.24	50.00	82243.03	1855.67	16325.21
27	4	93	616.82	67.11	50.00	82125.92	2472.49	16942.03
28	5	93	615.94	67.99	50.00	82007.93	3088.43	17557.97
29	6	93	615.06	68.87	50.00	81889.06	3703.49	18173.03

Pmt No.	Payment Mo	Payment Yr	Interest Portion	Principal Portion	Additional Principal	Remaining Loan Balance	Interest for Year	Cumulative Interest
30	7	93	614.17	69.76	50.00	81769.30	4317.66	18787.20
31	8	93	613.27	70.66	50.00	81648.64	4930.93	19400.47
32	9	93	612.36	71.57	50.00	81527.07	5543.29	20012.83
33	10	93	611.45	72.48	50.00	81404.59	6154.74	20624.28
34	11	93	610.53	73.40	50.00	81281.19	6765.27	21234.81
35	12	93	609.61	74.32	50.00	81156.87	7374.88	21844.42
36	1	94	608.68	75.25	50.00	81031.62	608.68	22453.10
37	2	94	607.74	76.19	50.00	80905.43	1216.42	23060.84
38	3	94	606.79	77.14	50.00	80778.29	1823.21	23667.63
39	4	94	605.84	78.09	50.00	80650.20	2429.05	24273.47
40	5	94	604.88	79.05	50.00	80521.15	3033.93	24878.35
41	6	94	603.91	80.02	50.00	80391.13	3637.84	25482.26
42	7	94	602.93	81.00	50.00	80260.13	4240.77	26085.19
43	8	94	601.95	81.98	50.00	80128.15	4842.72	26687.14
44	9	94	600.96	82.97	50.00	79995.18	5443.68	27288.10
45	10	94	599.96	83.97	50.00	79861.21	6043.64	27888.06
46	11	94	598.96	84.97	50.00	79726.24	6642.60	28487.02
47	12	94	597.95	85.98	50.00	79590.26	7240.55	29084.97
48	1	95	596.93	87.00	50.00	79453.26	596.93	29681.90
49	2	95	595.90	88.03	50.00	79315.23	1192.83	30277.80
50	3	95	594.86	89.07	50.00	79176.16	1787.69	30872.66
51	4	95	593.82	90.11	50.00	79036.05	2381.51	31466.48
52	5	95	592.77	91.16	50.00	78894.89	2974.28	32059.25
53	6	95	591.71	92.22	50.00	78752.67	3565.99	32650.96
54	7	95	590.65	93.28	50.00	78609.39	4156.64	33241.61
55	8	95	589.57	94.36	50.00	78465.03	4746.21	33831.18
56	9	95	588.49	95.44	50.00	78319.59	5334.70	34419.67
57	10	95	587.40	96.53	50.00	78173.06	5922.10	35007.07
58	11	95	586.30	97.63	50.00	78025.43	6508.40	35593.37
59	12	95	585.19	98.74	50.00	77876.69	7093.59	36178.56
60	1	96	584.08	99.85	50.00	77726.84	584.08	36762.64
61	2	96	582.95	100.98	50.00	77575.86	1167.03	37345.59
62	3	96	581.82	102.11	50.00	77423.75	1748.85	37927.41
63	4	96	580.68	103.25	50.00	77270.50	2329.53	38508.09
64	5	96	579.53	104.40	50.00	77116.10	2909.06	39087.62
65	6	96	578.37	105.56	50.00	76960.54	3487.43	39665.99
66	7	96	577.20	106.73	50.00	76803.81	4064.63	40243.19
67	8	96	576.03	107.90	50.00	76645.91	4640.66	40819.22
68	9	96	574.84	109.09	50.00	76486.82	5215.50	41394.06
69	10	96	573.65	110.28	50.00	76326.54	5789.15	41967.71
70	11	96	572.45	111.48	50.00	76165.06	6361.60	42540.16
71	12	96	571.24	112.69	50.00	76002.37	6932.84	43111.40
72	1	97	570.02	113.91	50.00	75838.46	570.02	43681.42
73	2	97	568.79	115.14	50.00	75673.32	1138.81	44250.21
74	3	97	567.55	116.38	50.00	75506.94	1706.36	44817.76
75	4	97	566.30	117.63	50.00	75339.31	2272.66	45384.06

Pmt No.	Payment Mo	Yr	Interest Portion	Principal Portion	Additional Principal	Remaining Loan Balance	Interest for Year	Cumulative Interest
76	5	97	565.04	118.89	50.00	75170.42	2837.70	45949.10
77	6	97	563.78	120.15	50.00	75000.27	3401.48	46512.88
78	7	97	562.50	121.43	50.00	74828.84	3963.98	47075.38
79	8	97	561.22	122.71	50.00	74656.13	4525.20	47636.60
80	9	97	559.92	124.01	50.00	74482.12	5085.12	48196.52
81	10	97	558.62	125.31	50.00	74306.81	5643.74	48755.14
82	11	97	557.30	126.63	50.00	74130.18	6201.04	49312.44
83	12	97	555.98	127.95	50.00	73952.23	6757.02	49868.42
84	1	98	554.64	129.29	50.00	73772.94	554.64	50423.06
85	2	98	553.30	130.63	50.00	73592.31	1107.94	50976.36
86	3	98	551.94	131.99	50.00	73410.32	1659.88	51528.30
87	4	98	550.58	133.35	50.00	73226.97	2210.46	52078.88
88	5	98	549.20	134.73	50.00	73042.24	2759.66	52628.08
89	6	98	547.82	136.11	50.00	72856.13	3307.48	53175.90
90	7	98	546.42	137.51	50.00	72668.62	3853.90	53722.32
91	8	98	545.01	138.92	50.00	72479.70	4398.91	54267.33
92	9	98	543.60	140.33	50.00	72289.37	4942.51	54810.93
93	10	98	542.17	141.76	50.00	72097.61	5484.68	55353.10
94	11	98	540.73	143.20	50.00	71904.41	6025.41	55893.83
95	12	98	539.28	144.65	50.00	71709.76	6564.69	56433.11
96	1	99	537.82	146.11	50.00	71513.65	537.82	56970.93
97	2	99	536.35	147.58	50.00	71316.07	1074.17	57507.28
98	3	99	534.87	149.06	50.00	71117.01	1609.04	58042.15
99	4	99	533.38	150.55	50.00	70916.46	2142.42	58575.53
100	5	99	531.87	152.06	50.00	70714.40	2674.29	59107.40
101	6	99	530.36	153.57	50.00	70510.83	3204.65	59637.76
102	7	99	528.83	155.10	50.00	70305.73	3733.48	60166.59
103	8	99	527.29	156.64	50.00	70099.09	4260.77	60693.88
104	9	99	525.74	158.19	50.00	69890.90	4786.51	61219.62
105	10	99	524.18	159.75	50.00	69681.15	5310.69	61743.80
106	11	99	522.61	161.32	50.00	69469.83	5833.30	62266.41
107	12	99	521.02	162.91	50.00	69256.92	6354.32	62787.43
108	1	0	519.43	164.50	50.00	69042.42	519.43	63306.86
109	2	0	517.82	166.11	50.00	68826.31	1037.25	63824.68
110	3	0	516.20	167.73	50.00	68608.58	1553.45	64340.88
111	4	0	514.56	169.37	50.00	68389.21	2068.01	64855.44
112	5	0	512.92	171.01	50.00	68168.20	2580.93	65368.36
113	6	0	511.26	172.67	50.00	67945.53	3092.19	65879.62
114	7	0	509.59	174.34	50.00	67721.19	3601.78	66389.21
115	8	0	507.91	176.02	50.00	67495.17	4109.69	66897.12
116	9	0	506.21	177.72	50.00	67267.45	4615.90	67403.33
117	10	0	504.51	179.42	50.00	67038.03	5120.41	67907.84
118	11	0	502.79	181.14	50.00	66806.89	5623.20	68410.63
119	12	0	501.05	182.88	50.00	66574.01	6124.25	68911.68
120	1	1	499.31	184.62	50.00	66339.39	499.31	69410.99
121	2	1	497.55	186.38	50.00	66103.01	996.86	69908.54

Pmt No.	Payment Mo	Yr	Interest Portion	Principal Portion	Additional Principal	Remaining Loan Balance	Interest for Year	Cumulative Interest
122	3	1	495.77	188.16	50.00	65864.85	1492.63	70404.31
123	4	1	493.99	189.94	50.00	65624.91	1986.62	70898.30
124	5	1	492.19	191.74	50.00	65383.17	2478.81	71390.49
125	6	1	490.37	193.56	50.00	65139.61	2969.18	71880.86
126	7	1	488.55	195.38	50.00	64894.23	3457.73	72369.41
127	8	1	486.71	197.22	50.00	64647.01	3944.44	72856.12
128	9	1	484.85	199.08	50.00	64397.93	4429.29	73340.97
129	10	1	482.98	200.95	50.00	64146.98	4912.27	73823.95
130	11	1	481.10	202.83	50.00	63894.15	5393.37	74305.05
131	12	1	479.21	204.72	50.00	63639.43	5872.58	74784.26
132	1	2	477.30	206.63	50.00	63382.80	477.30	75261.56
133	2	2	475.37	208.56	50.00	63124.24	952.67	75736.93
134	3	2	473.43	210.50	50.00	62863.74	1426.10	76210.36
135	4	2	471.48	212.45	50.00	62601.29	1897.58	76681.84
136	5	2	469.51	214.42	50.00	62336.87	2367.09	77151.35
137	6	2	467.53	216.40	50.00	62070.47	2834.62	77618.88
138	7	2	465.53	218.40	50.00	61802.07	3300.15	78084.41
139	8	2	463.52	220.41	50.00	61531.66	3763.67	78547.93
140	9	2	461.49	222.44	50.00	61259.22	4225.16	79009.42
141	10	2	459.44	224.49	50.00	60984.73	4684.60	79468.86
142	11	2	457.39	226.54	50.00	60708.19	5141.99	79926.25
143	12	2	455.31	228.62	50.00	60429.57	5597.30	80381.56
144	1	3	453.22	230.71	50.00	60148.86	453.22	80834.78
145	2	3	451.12	232.81	50.00	59866.05	904.34	81285.90
146	3	3	449.00	234.93	50.00	59581.12	1353.34	81734.90
147	4	3	446.86	237.07	50.00	59294.05	1800.20	82181.76
148	5	3	444.71	239.22	50.00	59004.83	2244.91	82626.47
149	6	3	442.54	241.39	50.00	58713.44	2687.45	83069.01
150	7	3	440.35	243.58	50.00	58419.86	3127.80	83509.36
151	8	3	438.15	245.78	50.00	58124.08	3565.95	83947.51
152	9	3	435.93	248.00	50.00	57826.08	4001.88	84383.44
153	10	3	433.70	250.23	50.00	57525.85	4435.58	84817.14
154	11	3	431.44	252.49	50.00	57223.36	4867.02	85248.58
155	12	3	429.18	254.75	50.00	56918.61	5296.20	85677.76
156	1	4	426.89	257.04	50.00	56611.57	426.89	86104.65
157	2	4	424.59	259.34	50.00	56302.23	851.48	86529.24
158	3	4	422.27	261.66	50.00	55990.57	1273.75	86951.51
159	4	4	419.93	264.00	50.00	55676.57	1693.68	87371.44
160	5	4	417.57	266.36	50.00	55360.21	2111.25	87789.01
161	6	4	415.20	268.73	50.00	55041.48	2526.45	88204.21
162	7	4	412.81	271.12	50.00	54720.36	2939.26	88617.02
163	8	4	410.40	273.53	50.00	54396.83	3349.66	89027.42
164	9	4	407.98	275.95	50.00	54070.88	3757.64	89435.40
165	10	4	405.53	278.40	50.00	53742.48	4163.17	89840.93
166	11	4	403.07	280.86	50.00	53411.62	4566.24	90244.00
167	12	4	400.59	283.34	50.00	53078.28	4966.83	90644.59

Pmt No.	Payment Mo	Yr	Interest Portion	Principal Portion	Additional Principal	Remaining Loan Balance	Interest for Year	Cumulative Interest
168	1	5	398.09	285.84	50.00	52742.44	398.09	91042.68
169	2	5	395.57	288.36	50.00	52404.08	793.66	91438.25
170	3	5	393.03	290.90	50.00	52063.18	1186.69	91831.28
171	4	5	390.47	293.46	50.00	51719.72	1577.16	92221.75
172	5	5	387.90	296.03	50.00	51373.69	1965.06	92609.65
173	6	5	385.30	298.63	50.00	51025.06	2350.36	92994.95
174	7	5	382.69	301.24	50.00	50673.82	2733.05	93377.64
175	8	5	380.05	303.88	50.00	50319.94	3113.10	93757.69
176	9	5	377.40	306.53	50.00	49963.41	3490.50	94135.09
177	10	5	374.73	309.20	50.00	49604.21	3865.23	94509.82
178	11	5	372.03	311.90	50.00	49242.31	4237.26	94881.85
179	12	5	369.32	314.61	50.00	48877.70	4606.58	95251.17
180	1	6	366.58	317.35	50.00	48510.35	366.58	95617.75
181	2	6	363.83	320.10	50.00	48140.25	730.41	95981.58
182	3	6	361.05	322.88	50.00	47767.37	1091.46	96342.63
183	4	6	358.26	325.67	50.00	47391.70	1449.72	96700.89
184	5	6	355.44	328.49	50.00	47013.21	1805.16	97056.33
185	6	6	352.60	331.33	50.00	46631.88	2157.76	97408.93
186	7	6	349.74	334.19	50.00	46247.69	2507.50	97758.67
187	8	6	346.86	337.07	50.00	45860.62	2854.36	98105.53
188	9	6	343.95	339.98	50.00	45470.64	3198.31	98449.48
189	10	6	341.03	342.90	50.00	45077.74	3539.34	98790.51
190	11	6	338.08	345.85	50.00	44681.89	3877.42	99128.59
191	12	6	335.11	348.82	50.00	44283.07	4212.53	99463.70
192	1	7	332.12	351.81	50.00	43881.26	332.12	99795.82
193	2	7	329.11	354.82	50.00	43476.44	661.23	100124.93
194	3	7	326.07	357.86	50.00	43068.58	987.30	100451.00
195	4	7	323.01	360.92	50.00	42657.66	1310.31	100774.01
196	5	7	319.93	364.00	50.00	42243.66	1630.24	101093.94
197	6	7	316.83	367.10	50.00	41826.56	1947.07	101410.77
198	7	7	313.70	370.23	50.00	41406.33	2260.77	101724.47
199	8	7	310.55	373.38	50.00	40982.95	2571.32	102035.02
200	9	7	307.37	376.56	50.00	40556.39	2878.69	102342.39
201	10	7	304.17	379.76	50.00	40126.63	3182.86	102646.56
202	11	7	300.95	382.98	50.00	39693.65	3483.81	102947.51
203	12	7	297.70	386.23	50.00	39257.42	3781.51	103245.21
204	1	8	294.43	389.50	50.00	38817.92	294.43	103539.64
205	2	8	291.13	392.80	50.00	38375.12	585.56	103830.77
206	3	8	287.81	396.12	50.00	37929.00	873.37	104118.58
207	4	8	284.47	399.46	50.00	37479.54	1157.84	104403.05
208	5	8	281.10	402.83	50.00	37026.71	1438.94	104684.15
209	6	8	277.70	406.23	50.00	36570.48	1716.64	104961.85
210	7	8	274.28	409.65	50.00	36110.83	1990.92	105236.13
211	8	8	270.83	413.10	50.00	35647.73	2261.75	105506.96
212	9	8	267.36	416.57	50.00	35181.16	2529.11	105774.32
213	10	8	263.86	420.07	50.00	34711.09	2792.97	106038.18

Pmt No.	Payment Mo	Yr	Interest Portion	Principal Portion	Additional Principal	Remaining Loan Balance	Interest for Year	Cumulative Interest
214	11	8	260.33	423.60	50.00	34237.49	3053.30	106298.51
215	12	8	256.78	427.15	50.00	33760.34	3310.08	106555.29
216	1	9	253.20	430.73	50.00	33279.61	253.20	106808.49
217	2	9	249.60	434.33	50.00	32795.28	502.80	107058.09
218	3	9	245.96	437.97	50.00	32307.31	748.76	107304.05
219	4	9	242.30	441.63	50.00	31815.68	991.06	107546.35
220	5	9	238.62	445.31	50.00	31320.37	1229.68	107784.97
221	6	9	234.90	449.03	50.00	30821.34	1464.58	108019.87
222	7	9	231.16	452.77	50.00	30318.57	1695.74	108251.03
223	8	9	227.39	456.54	50.00	29812.03	1923.13	108478.42
224	9	9	223.59	460.34	50.00	29301.69	2146.72	108702.01
225	10	9	219.76	464.17	50.00	28787.52	2366.48	108921.77
226	11	9	215.91	468.02	50.00	28269.50	2582.39	109137.68
227	12	9	212.02	471.91	50.00	27747.59	2794.41	109349.70
228	1	10	208.11	475.82	50.00	27221.77	208.11	109557.81
229	2	10	204.16	479.77	50.00	26692.00	412.27	109761.97
230	3	10	200.19	483.74	50.00	26158.26	612.46	109962.16
231	4	10	196.19	487.74	50.00	25620.52	808.65	110158.35
232	5	10	192.15	491.78	50.00	25078.74	1000.80	110350.50
233	6	10	188.09	495.84	50.00	24532.90	1188.89	110538.59
234	7	10	184.00	499.93	50.00	23982.97	1372.89	110722.59
235	8	10	179.87	504.06	50.00	23428.91	1552.76	110902.46
236	9	10	175.72	508.21	50.00	22870.70	1728.48	111078.18
237	10	10	171.53	512.40	50.00	22308.30	1900.01	111249.71
238	11	10	167.31	516.62	50.00	21741.68	2067.32	111417.02
239	12	10	163.06	520.87	50.00	21170.81	2230.38	111580.08
240	1	11	158.78	525.15	50.00	20595.66	158.78	111738.86
241	2	11	154.47	529.46	50.00	20016.20	313.25	111893.33
242	3	11	150.12	533.81	50.00	19432.39	463.37	112043.45
243	4	11	145.74	538.19	50.00	18844.20	609.11	112189.19
244	5	11	141.33	542.60	50.00	18251.60	750.44	112330.52
245	6	11	136.89	547.04	50.00	17654.56	887.33	112467.41
246	7	11	132.41	551.52	50.00	17053.04	1019.74	112599.82
247	8	11	127.90	556.03	50.00	16447.01	1147.64	112727.72
248	9	11	123.35	560.58	50.00	15836.43	1270.99	112851.07
249	10	11	118.77	565.16	50.00	15221.27	1389.76	112969.84
250	11	11	114.16	569.77	50.00	14601.50	1503.92	113084.00
251	12	11	109.51	574.42	50.00	13977.08	1613.43	113193.51
252	1	12	104.83	579.10	50.00	13347.98	104.83	113298.34
253	2	12	100.11	583.82	50.00	12714.16	204.94	113398.45
254	3	12	95.36	588.57	50.00	12075.59	300.30	113493.81
255	4	12	90.57	593.36	50.00	11432.23	390.87	113584.38
256	5	12	85.74	598.19	50.00	10784.04	476.61	113670.12
257	6	12	80.88	603.05	50.00	10130.99	557.49	113751.00
258	7	12	75.98	607.95	50.00	9473.04	633.47	113826.98
259	8	12	71.05	612.88	50.00	8810.16	704.52	113898.03

Pmt No.	Payment Mo	Yr	Interest Portion	Principal Portion	Additional Principal	Remaining Loan Balance	Interest for Year	Cumulative Interest
260	9	12	66.08	617.85	50.00	8142.31	770.60	113964.11
261	10	12	61.07	622.86	50.00	7469.45	831.67	114025.18
262	11	12	56.02	627.91	50.00	6791.54	887.69	114081.20
263	12	12	50.94	632.99	50.00	6108.55	938.63	114132.14
264	1	13	45.81	638.12	50.00	5420.43	45.81	114177.95
265	2	13	40.65	643.28	50.00	4727.15	86.46	114218.60
266	3	13	35.45	648.48	50.00	4028.67	121.91	114254.05
267	4	13	30.22	653.71	50.00	3324.96	152.13	114284.27
268	5	13	24.94	658.99	50.00	2615.97	177.07	114309.21
269	6	13	19.62	664.31	50.00	1901.66	196.69	114328.83
270	7	13	14.26	669.67	50.00	1181.99	210.95	114343.09
271	8	13	8.86	675.07	50.00	456.92	219.81	114351.95
272	9	13	3.43	456.92	0.00	0.00	223.24	114355.38

Loan Account Information

Name:	Gary Sanseri
Address:	8431 S.E. 36th Ave.
City, State ZIP:	Portland, OR 97222
Telephone:	505-654-2300
Reference:	Loan No. 50637

Loan Data

Original Loan Amount:	85000.00
Original Loan Date (mo.yr):	1.91
Annual Interest Rate:	9.00
Original Loan Period - Months:	360
User Entered Monthly Payment:	
Calculated Monthly Loan Payment:	683.93
Total Calculated Payments:	246214.80
Total Calculated Interest:	161214.80

sample loan with $100 prepayment

Pmt No.	Mo	Yr	Interest Portion	Principal Portion	Additional Principal	Remaining Loan Balance	Interest for Year	Cumulative Interest
1	2	91	637.50	46.43	100.00	84853.57	637.50	637.5
2	3	91	636.40	47.53	100.00	84706.04	1273.90	1273.90
3	4	91	635.30	48.63	100.00	84557.41	1909.20	1909.20
4	5	91	634.18	49.75	100.00	84407.66	2543.38	2543.38
5	6	91	633.06	50.87	100.00	84256.79	3176.44	3176.44
6	7	91	631.93	52.00	100.00	84104.79	3808.37	3808.37
7	8	91	630.79	53.14	100.00	83951.65	4439.16	4439.16
8	9	91	629.64	54.29	100.00	83797.36	5068.80	5068.80
9	10	91	628.48	55.45	100.00	83641.91	5697.28	5697.28
10	11	91	627.31	56.62	100.00	83485.29	6324.59	6324.59
11	12	91	626.14	57.79	100.00	83327.50	6950.73	6950.73
12	1	92	624.96	58.97	100.00	83168.53	624.96	7575.69
13	2	92	623.76	60.17	100.00	83008.36	1248.72	8199.45
14	3	92	622.56	61.37	100.00	82846.99	1871.28	8822.01
15	4	92	621.35	62.58	100.00	82684.41	2492.63	9443.36
16	5	92	620.13	63.80	100.00	82520.61	3112.76	10063.49
17	6	92	618.90	65.03	100.00	82355.58	3731.66	10682.39
18	7	92	617.67	66.26	100.00	82189.32	4349.33	11300.06
19	8	92	616.42	67.51	100.00	82021.81	4965.75	11916.48
20	9	92	615.16	68.77	100.00	81853.04	5580.91	12531.64
21	10	92	613.90	70.03	100.00	81683.01	6194.81	13145.54
22	11	92	612.62	71.31	100.00	81511.70	6807.43	13758.16
23	12	92	611.34	72.59	100.00	81339.11	7418.77	14369.50
24	1	93	610.04	73.89	100.00	81165.22	610.04	14979.54
25	2	93	608.74	75.19	100.00	80990.03	1218.78	15588.28
26	3	93	607.43	76.50	100.00	80813.53	1826.21	16195.71
27	4	93	606.10	77.83	100.00	80635.70	2432.31	16801.81
28	5	93	604.77	79.16	100.00	80456.54	3037.08	17406.58
29	6	93	603.42	80.51	100.00	80276.03	3640.50	18010.00

Pmt No.	Payment Mo	Payment Yr	Interest Portion	Principal Portion	Additional Principal	Remaining Loan Balance	Interest for Year	Cumulative Interest
30	7	93	602.07	81.86	100.00	80094.17	4242.57	18612.07
31	8	93	600.71	83.22	100.00	79910.95	4843.28	19212.78
32	9	93	599.33	84.60	100.00	79726.35	5442.61	19812.11
33	10	93	597.95	85.98	100.00	79540.37	6040.56	20410.06
34	11	93	596.55	87.38	100.00	79352.99	6637.11	21006.61
35	12	93	595.15	88.78	100.00	79164.21	7232.26	21601.76
36	1	94	593.73	90.20	100.00	78974.01	593.73	22195.49
37	2	94	592.31	91.62	100.00	78782.39	1186.04	22787.80
38	3	94	590.87	93.06	100.00	78589.33	1776.91	23378.67
39	4	94	589.42	94.51	100.00	78394.82	2366.33	23968.09
40	5	94	587.96	95.97	100.00	78198.85	2954.29	24556.05
41	6	94	586.49	97.44	100.00	78001.41	3540.78	25142.54
42	7	94	585.01	98.92	100.00	77802.49	4125.79	25727.55
43	8	94	583.52	100.41	100.00	77602.08	4709.31	26311.07
44	9	94	582.02	101.91	100.00	77400.17	5291.33	26893.09
45	10	94	580.50	103.43	100.00	77196.74	5871.83	27473.59
46	11	94	578.98	104.95	100.00	76991.79	6450.81	28052.57
47	12	94	577.44	106.49	100.00	76785.30	7028.25	28630.01
48	1	95	575.89	108.04	100.00	76577.26	575.89	29205.90
49	2	95	574.33	109.60	100.00	76367.66	1150.22	29780.23
50	3	95	572.76	111.17	100.00	76156.49	1722.98	30352.99
51	4	95	571.17	112.76	100.00	75943.73	2294.15	30924.16
52	5	95	569.58	114.35	100.00	75729.38	2863.73	31493.74
53	6	95	567.97	115.96	100.00	75513.42	3431.70	32061.71
54	7	95	566.35	117.58	100.00	75295.84	3998.05	32628.06
55	8	95	564.72	119.21	100.00	75076.63	4562.77	33192.78
56	9	95	563.07	120.86	100.00	74855.77	5125.84	33755.85
57	10	95	561.42	122.51	100.00	74633.26	5687.26	34317.27
58	11	95	559.75	124.18	100.00	74409.08	6247.01	34877.02
59	12	95	558.07	125.86	100.00	74183.22	6805.08	35435.09
60	1	96	556.37	127.56	100.00	73955.66	556.37	35991.46
61	2	96	554.67	129.26	100.00	73726.40	1111.04	36546.13
62	3	96	552.95	130.98	100.00	73495.42	1663.99	37099.08
63	4	96	551.22	132.71	100.00	73262.71	2215.21	37650.30
64	5	96	549.47	134.46	100.00	73028.25	2764.68	38199.77
65	6	96	547.71	136.22	100.00	72792.03	3312.39	38747.48
66	7	96	545.94	137.99	100.00	72554.04	3858.33	39293.42
67	8	96	544.16	139.77	100.00	72314.27	4402.49	39837.58
68	9	96	542.36	141.57	100.00	72072.70	4944.85	40379.94
69	10	96	540.55	143.38	100.00	71829.32	5485.40	40920.49
70	11	96	538.72	145.21	100.00	71584.11	6024.12	41459.21
71	12	96	536.88	147.05	100.00	71337.06	6561.00	41996.09
72	1	97	535.03	148.90	100.00	71088.16	535.03	42531.12
73	2	97	533.16	150.77	100.00	70837.39	1068.19	43064.28
74	3	97	531.28	152.65	100.00	70584.74	1599.47	43595.56
75	4	97	529.39	154.54	100.00	70330.20	2128.86	44124.95

Pmt No.	Payment Mo	Yr	Interest Portion	Principal Portion	Additional Principal	Remaining Loan Balance	Interest for Year	Cumulative Interest
76	5	97	527.48	156.45	100.00	70073.75	2656.34	44652.43
77	6	97	525.55	158.38	100.00	69815.37	3181.89	45177.98
78	7	97	523.62	160.31	100.00	69555.06	3705.51	45701.60
79	8	97	521.66	162.27	100.00	69292.79	4227.17	46223.26
80	9	97	519.70	164.23	100.00	69028.56	4746.87	46742.96
81	10	97	517.71	166.22	100.00	68762.34	5264.58	47260.67
82	11	97	515.72	168.21	100.00	68494.13	5780.30	47776.39
83	12	97	513.71	170.22	100.00	68223.91	6294.01	48290.10
84	1	98	511.68	172.25	100.00	67951.66	511.68	48801.78
85	2	98	509.64	174.29	100.00	67677.37	1021.32	49311.42
86	3	98	507.58	176.35	100.00	67401.02	1528.90	49819.00
87	4	98	505.51	178.42	100.00	67122.60	2034.41	50324.51
88	5	98	503.42	180.51	100.00	66842.09	2537.83	50827.93
89	6	98	501.32	182.61	100.00	66559.48	3039.15	51329.25
90	7	98	499.20	184.73	100.00	66274.75	3538.35	51828.45
91	8	98	497.06	186.87	100.00	65987.88	4035.41	52325.51
92	9	98	494.91	189.02	100.00	65698.86	4530.32	52820.42
93	10	98	492.74	191.19	100.00	65407.67	5023.06	53313.16
94	11	98	490.56	193.37	100.00	65114.30	5513.62	53803.72
95	12	98	488.36	195.57	100.00	64818.73	6001.98	54292.08
96	1	99	486.14	197.79	100.00	64520.94	486.14	54778.22
97	2	99	483.91	200.02	100.00	64220.92	970.05	55262.13
98	3	99	481.66	202.27	100.00	63918.65	1451.71	55743.79
99	4	99	479.39	204.54	100.00	63614.11	1931.10	56223.18
100	5	99	477.11	206.82	100.00	63307.29	2408.21	56700.29
101	6	99	474.80	209.13	100.00	62998.16	2883.01	57175.09
102	7	99	472.49	211.44	100.00	62686.72	3355.50	57647.58
103	8	99	470.15	213.78	100.00	62372.94	3825.65	58117.73
104	9	99	467.80	216.13	100.00	62056.81	4293.45	58585.53
105	10	99	465.43	218.50	100.00	61738.31	4758.88	59050.96
106	11	99	463.04	220.89	100.00	61417.42	5221.92	59514.00
107	12	99	460.63	223.30	100.00	61094.12	5682.55	59974.63
108	1	0	458.21	225.72	100.00	60768.40	458.21	60432.84
109	2	0	455.76	228.17	100.00	60440.23	913.97	60888.60
110	3	0	453.30	230.63	100.00	60109.60	1367.27	61341.90
111	4	0	450.82	233.11	100.00	59776.49	1818.09	61792.72
112	5	0	448.32	235.61	100.00	59440.88	2266.41	62241.04
113	6	0	445.81	238.12	100.00	59102.76	2712.22	62686.85
114	7	0	443.27	240.66	100.00	58762.10	3155.49	63130.12
115	8	0	440.72	243.21	100.00	58418.89	3596.21	63570.84
116	9	0	438.14	245.79	100.00	58073.10	4034.35	64008.98
117	10	0	435.55	248.38	100.00	57724.72	4469.90	64444.53
118	11	0	432.94	250.99	100.00	57373.73	4902.84	64877.47
119	12	0	430.30	253.63	100.00	57020.10	5333.14	65307.77
120	1	1	427.65	256.28	100.00	56663.82	427.65	65735.42
121	2	1	424.98	258.95	100.00	56304.87	852.63	66160.40

Pmt No.	Payment Mo	Yr	Interest Portion	Principal Portion	Additional Principal	Remaining Loan Balance	Interest for Year	Cumulative Interest
122	3	1	422.29	261.64	100.00	55943.23	1274.92	66582.69
123	4	1	419.57	264.36	100.00	55578.87	1694.49	67002.26
124	5	1	416.84	267.09	100.00	55211.78	2111.33	67419.10
125	6	1	414.09	269.84	100.00	54841.94	2525.42	67833.19
126	7	1	411.31	272.62	100.00	54469.32	2936.73	68244.50
127	8	1	408.52	275.41	100.00	54093.91	3345.25	68653.02
128	9	1	405.70	278.23	100.00	53715.68	3750.95	69058.72
129	10	1	402.87	281.06	100.00	53334.62	4153.82	69461.59
130	11	1	400.01	283.92	100.00	52950.70	4553.83	69861.60
131	12	1	397.13	286.80	100.00	52563.90	4950.96	70258.73
132	1	2	394.23	289.70	100.00	52174.20	394.23	70652.96
133	2	2	391.31	292.62	100.00	51781.58	785.54	71044.27
134	3	2	388.36	295.57	100.00	51386.01	1173.90	71432.63
135	4	2	385.40	298.53	100.00	50987.48	1559.30	71818.03
136	5	2	382.41	301.52	100.00	50585.96	1941.71	72200.44
137	6	2	379.39	304.54	100.00	50181.42	2321.10	72579.83
138	7	2	376.36	307.57	100.00	49773.85	2697.46	72956.19
139	8	2	373.30	310.63	100.00	49363.22	3070.76	73329.49
140	9	2	370.22	313.71	100.00	48949.51	3440.98	73699.71
141	10	2	367.12	316.81	100.00	48532.70	3808.10	74066.83
142	11	2	364.00	319.93	100.00	48112.77	4172.10	74430.83
143	12	2	360.85	323.08	100.00	47689.69	4532.95	74791.68
144	1	3	357.67	326.26	100.00	47263.43	357.67	75149.35
145	2	3	354.48	329.45	100.00	46833.98	712.15	75503.83
146	3	3	351.25	332.68	100.00	46401.30	1063.40	75855.08
147	4	3	348.01	335.92	100.00	45965.38	1411.41	76203.09
148	5	3	344.74	339.19	100.00	45526.19	1756.15	76547.83
149	6	3	341.45	342.48	100.00	45083.71	2097.60	76889.28
150	7	3	338.13	345.80	100.00	44637.91	2435.73	77227.41
151	8	3	334.78	349.15	100.00	44188.76	2770.51	77562.19
152	9	3	331.42	352.51	100.00	43736.25	3101.93	77893.61
153	10	3	328.02	355.91	100.00	43280.34	3429.95	78221.63
154	11	3	324.60	359.33	100.00	42821.01	3754.55	78546.23
155	12	3	321.16	362.77	100.00	42358.24	4075.71	78867.39
156	1	4	317.69	366.24	100.00	41892.00	317.69	79185.08
157	2	4	314.19	369.74	100.00	41422.26	631.88	79499.27
158	3	4	310.67	373.26	100.00	40949.00	942.55	79809.94
159	4	4	307.12	376.81	100.00	40472.19	1249.67	80117.06
160	5	4	303.54	380.39	100.00	39991.80	1553.21	80420.60
161	6	4	299.94	383.99	100.00	39507.81	1853.15	80720.54
162	7	4	296.31	387.62	100.00	39020.19	2149.46	81016.85
163	8	4	292.65	391.28	100.00	38528.91	2442.11	81309.50
164	9	4	288.97	394.96	100.00	38033.95	2731.08	81598.47
165	10	4	285.25	398.68	100.00	37535.27	3016.33	81883.72
166	11	4	281.51	402.42	100.00	37032.85	3297.84	82165.23
167	12	4	277.75	406.18	100.00	36526.67	3575.59	82442.98

Pmt No.	Payment Mo	Yr	Interest Portion	Principal Portion	Additional Principal	Remaining Loan Balance	Interest for Year	Cumulative Interest
168	1	5	273.95	409.98	100.00	36016.69	273.95	82716.93
169	2	5	270.13	413.80	100.00	35502.89	544.08	82987.06
170	3	5	266.27	417.66	100.00	34985.23	810.35	83253.33
171	4	5	262.39	421.54	100.00	34463.69	1072.74	83515.72
172	5	5	258.48	425.45	100.00	33938.24	1331.22	83774.20
173	6	5	254.54	429.39	100.00	33408.85	1585.76	84028.74
174	7	5	250.57	433.36	100.00	32875.49	1836.33	84279.31
175	8	5	246.57	437.36	100.00	32338.13	2082.90	84525.88
176	9	5	242.54	441.39	100.00	31796.74	2325.44	84768.42
177	10	5	238.48	445.45	100.00	31251.29	2563.92	85006.90
178	11	5	234.38	449.55	100.00	30701.74	2798.30	85241.28
179	12	5	230.26	453.67	100.00	30148.07	3028.56	85471.54
180	1	6	226.11	457.82	100.00	29590.25	226.11	85697.65
181	2	6	221.93	462.00	100.00	29028.25	448.04	85919.58
182	3	6	217.71	466.22	100.00	28462.03	665.75	86137.29
183	4	6	213.47	470.46	100.00	27891.57	879.22	86350.76
184	5	6	209.19	474.74	100.00	27316.83	1088.41	86559.95
185	6	6	204.88	479.05	100.00	26737.78	1293.29	86764.83
186	7	6	200.53	483.40	100.00	26154.38	1493.82	86965.36
187	8	6	196.16	487.77	100.00	25566.61	1689.98	87161.52
188	9	6	191.75	492.18	100.00	24974.43	1881.73	87353.27
189	10	6	187.31	496.62	100.00	24377.81	2069.04	87540.58
190	11	6	182.83	501.10	100.00	23776.71	2251.87	87723.41
191	12	6	178.33	505.60	100.00	23171.11	2430.20	87901.74
192	1	7	173.78	510.15	100.00	22560.96	173.78	88075.52
193	2	7	169.21	514.72	100.00	21946.24	342.99	88244.73
194	3	7	164.60	519.33	100.00	21326.91	507.59	88409.33
195	4	7	159.95	523.98	100.00	20702.93	667.54	88569.28
196	5	7	155.27	528.66	100.00	20074.27	822.81	88724.55
197	6	7	150.56	533.37	100.00	19440.90	973.37	88875.11
198	7	7	145.81	538.12	100.00	18802.78	1119.18	89020.92
199	8	7	141.02	542.91	100.00	18159.87	1260.20	89161.94
200	9	7	136.20	547.73	100.00	17512.14	1396.40	89298.14
201	10	7	131.34	552.59	100.00	16859.55	1527.74	89429.48
202	11	7	126.45	557.48	100.00	16202.07	1654.19	89555.93
203	12	7	121.52	562.41	100.00	15539.66	1775.71	89677.45
204	1	8	116.55	567.38	100.00	14872.28	116.55	89794.00
205	2	8	111.54	572.39	100.00	14199.89	228.09	89905.54
206	3	8	106.50	577.43	100.00	13522.46	334.59	90012.04
207	4	8	101.42	582.51	100.00	12839.95	436.01	90113.46
208	5	8	96.30	587.63	100.00	12152.32	532.31	90209.76
209	6	8	91.14	592.79	100.00	11459.53	623.45	90300.90
210	7	8	85.95	597.98	100.00	10761.55	709.40	90386.85
211	8	8	80.71	603.22	100.00	10058.33	790.11	90467.56
212	9	8	75.44	608.49	100.00	9349.84	865.55	90543.00
213	10	8	70.12	613.81	100.00	8636.03	935.67	90613.12

Pmt No.	Payment Mo	Payment Yr	Interest Portion	Principal Portion	Additional Principal	Remaining Loan Balance	Interest for Year	Cumulative Interest
214	11	8	64.77	619.16	100.00	7916.87	1000.44	90677.89
215	12	8	59.38	624.55	100.00	7192.32	1059.82	90737.27
216	1	9	53.94	629.99	100.00	6462.33	53.94	90791.21
217	2	9	48.47	635.46	100.00	5726.87	102.41	90839.68
218	3	9	42.95	640.98	100.00	4985.89	145.36	90882.63
219	4	9	37.39	646.54	100.00	4239.35	182.75	90920.02
220	5	9	31.80	652.13	100.00	3487.22	214.55	90951.82
221	6	9	26.15	657.78	100.00	2729.44	240.70	90977.97
222	7	9	20.47	663.46	100.00	1965.98	261.17	90998.44
223	8	9	14.74	669.19	100.00	1196.79	275.91	91013.18
224	9	9	8.98	674.95	100.00	421.84	284.89	91022.16
225	10	9	3.16	421.84	0.00	0.00	288.05	91025.32

Loan Account Information

Name:	Gary Sanseri
Address:	8431 S.E. 36th Ave.
City, State ZIP:	Portland, OR 97222
Telephone:	505-654-2300
Reference:	Loan No. 50637

Loan Data

Original Loan Amount:	85000.00
Original Loan Date (mo.yr):	1.91
Annual Interest Rate:	9.00
Original Loan Period - Months:	360
User Entered Monthly Payment:	
Calculated Monthly Loan Payment:	683.93
Total Calculated Payments:	246214.80
Total Calculated Interest:	161214.80

sample loan with $200 prepayment

Pmt No.	Payment Mo	Yr	Interest Portion	Principal Portion	Additional Principal	Remaining Loan Balance	Interest for Year	Cumulative Interest
1	2	91	637.50	46.43	200.00	84753.57	637.50	637.5
2	3	91	635.65	48.28	200.00	84505.29	1273.15	1273.15
3	4	91	633.79	50.14	200.00	84255.15	1906.94	1906.94
4	5	91	631.91	52.02	200.00	84003.13	2538.85	2538.85
5	6	91	630.02	53.91	200.00	83749.22	3168.87	3168.87
6	7	91	628.12	55.81	200.00	83493.41	3796.99	3796.99
7	8	91	626.20	57.73	200.00	83235.68	4423.19	4423.19
8	9	91	624.27	59.66	200.00	82976.02	5047.46	5047.46
9	10	91	622.32	61.61	200.00	82714.41	5669.78	5669.78
10	11	91	620.36	63.57	200.00	82450.84	6290.14	6290.14
11	12	91	618.38	65.55	200.00	82185.29	6908.52	6908.52
12	1	92	616.39	67.54	200.00	81917.75	616.39	7524.91
13	2	92	614.38	69.55	200.00	81648.20	1230.77	8139.29
14	3	92	612.36	71.57	200.00	81376.63	1843.13	8751.65
15	4	92	610.32	73.61	200.00	81103.02	2453.45	9361.97
16	5	92	608.27	75.66	200.00	80827.36	3061.72	9970.24
17	6	92	606.21	77.72	200.00	80549.64	3667.93	10576.45
18	7	92	604.12	79.81	200.00	80269.83	4272.05	11180.57
19	8	92	602.02	81.91	200.00	79987.92	4874.07	11782.59
20	9	92	599.91	84.02	200.00	79703.90	5473.98	12382.50
21	10	92	597.78	86.15	200.00	79417.75	6071.76	12980.28
22	11	92	595.63	88.30	200.00	79129.45	6667.39	13575.91
23	12	92	593.47	90.46	200.00	78838.99	7260.86	14169.38
24	1	93	591.29	92.64	200.00	78546.35	591.29	14760.67
25	2	93	589.10	94.83	200.00	78251.52	1180.39	15349.77
26	3	93	586.89	97.04	200.00	77954.48	1767.28	15936.66
27	4	93	584.66	99.27	200.00	77655.21	2351.94	16521.32
28	5	93	582.41	101.52	200.00	77353.69	2934.35	17103.73
29	6	93	580.15	103.78	200.00	77049.91	3514.50	17683.88

Pmt No.	Payment Mo	Yr	Interest Portion	Principal Portion	Additional Principal	Remaining Loan Balance	Interest for Year	Cumulative Interest
30	7	93	577.87	106.06	200.00	76743.85	4092.37	18261.75
31	8	93	575.58	108.35	200.00	76435.50	4667.95	18837.33
32	9	93	573.27	110.66	200.00	76124.84	5241.22	19410.60
33	10	93	570.94	112.99	200.00	75811.85	5812.16	19981.54
34	11	93	568.59	115.34	200.00	75496.51	6380.75	20550.13
35	12	93	566.22	117.71	200.00	75178.80	6946.97	21116.35
36	1	94	563.84	120.09	200.00	74858.71	563.84	21680.19
37	2	94	561.44	122.49	200.00	74536.22	1125.28	22241.63
38	3	94	559.02	124.91	200.00	74211.31	1684.30	22800.65
39	4	94	556.58	127.35	200.00	73883.96	2240.88	23357.23
40	5	94	554.13	129.80	200.00	73554.16	2795.01	23911.36
41	6	94	551.66	132.27	200.00	73221.89	3346.67	24463.02
42	7	94	549.16	134.77	200.00	72887.12	3895.83	25012.18
43	8	94	546.65	137.28	200.00	72549.84	4442.48	25558.83
44	9	94	544.12	139.81	200.00	72210.03	4986.60	26102.95
45	10	94	541.58	142.35	200.00	71867.68	5528.18	26644.53
46	11	94	539.01	144.92	200.00	71522.76	6067.19	27183.54
47	12	94	536.42	147.51	200.00	71175.25	6603.61	27719.96
48	1	95	533.81	150.12	200.00	70825.13	533.81	28253.77
49	2	95	531.19	152.74	200.00	70472.39	1065.00	28784.96
50	3	95	528.54	155.39	200.00	70117.00	1593.54	29313.50
51	4	95	525.88	158.05	200.00	69758.95	2119.42	29839.38
52	5	95	523.19	160.74	200.00	69398.21	2642.61	30362.57
53	6	95	520.49	163.44	200.00	69034.77	3163.10	30883.06
54	7	95	517.76	166.17	200.00	68668.60	3680.86	31400.82
55	8	95	515.01	168.92	200.00	68299.68	4195.87	31915.83
56	9	95	512.25	171.68	200.00	67928.00	4708.12	32428.08
57	10	95	509.46	174.47	200.00	67553.53	5217.58	32937.54
58	11	95	506.65	177.28	200.00	67176.25	5724.23	33444.19
59	12	95	503.82	180.11	200.00	66796.14	6228.05	33948.01
60	1	96	500.97	182.96	200.00	66413.18	500.97	34448.98
61	2	96	498.10	185.83	200.00	66027.35	999.07	34947.08
62	3	96	495.21	188.72	200.00	65638.63	1494.28	35442.29
63	4	96	492.29	191.64	200.00	65246.99	1986.57	35934.58
64	5	96	489.35	194.58	200.00	64852.41	2475.92	36423.93
65	6	96	486.39	197.54	200.00	64454.87	2962.31	36910.32
66	7	96	483.41	200.52	200.00	64054.35	3445.72	37393.73
67	8	96	480.41	203.52	200.00	63650.83	3926.13	37874.14
68	9	96	477.38	206.55	200.00	63244.28	4403.51	38351.52
69	10	96	474.33	209.60	200.00	62834.68	4877.84	38825.85
70	11	96	471.26	212.67	200.00	62422.01	5349.10	39297.11
71	12	96	468.17	215.76	200.00	62006.25	5817.27	39765.28
72	1	97	465.05	218.88	200.00	61587.37	465.05	40230.33
73	2	97	461.91	222.02	200.00	61165.35	926.96	40692.24
74	3	97	458.74	225.19	200.00	60740.16	1385.70	41150.98
75	4	97	455.55	228.38	200.00	60311.78	1841.25	41606.53

Pmt No.	Payment Mo	Yr	Interest Portion	Principal Portion	Additional Principal	Remaining Loan Balance	Interest for Year	Cumulative Interest
76	5	97	452.34	231.59	200.00	59880.19	2293.59	42058.87
77	6	97	449.10	234.83	200.00	59445.36	2742.69	42507.97
78	7	97	445.84	238.09	200.00	59007.27	3188.53	42953.81
79	8	97	442.55	241.38	200.00	58565.89	3631.08	43396.36
80	9	97	439.24	244.69	200.00	58121.20	4070.32	43835.60
81	10	97	435.91	248.02	200.00	57673.18	4506.23	44271.51
82	11	97	432.55	251.38	200.00	57221.80	4938.78	44704.06
83	12	97	429.16	254.77	200.00	56767.03	5367.94	45133.22
84	1	98	425.75	258.18	200.00	56308.85	425.75	45558.97
85	2	98	422.32	261.61	200.00	55847.24	848.07	45981.29
86	3	98	418.85	265.08	200.00	55382.16	1266.92	46400.14
87	4	98	415.37	268.56	200.00	54913.60	1682.29	46815.51
88	5	98	411.85	272.08	200.00	54441.52	2094.14	47227.36
89	6	98	408.31	275.62	200.00	53965.90	2502.45	47635.67
90	7	98	404.74	279.19	200.00	53486.71	2907.19	48040.41
91	8	98	401.15	282.78	200.00	53003.93	3308.34	48441.56
92	9	98	397.53	286.40	200.00	52517.53	3705.87	48839.09
93	10	98	393.88	290.05	200.00	52027.48	4099.75	49232.97
94	11	98	390.21	293.72	200.00	51533.76	4489.96	49623.18
95	12	98	386.50	297.43	200.00	51036.33	4876.46	50009.68
96	1	99	382.77	301.16	200.00	50535.17	382.77	50392.45
97	2	99	379.01	304.92	200.00	50030.25	761.78	50771.46
98	3	99	375.23	308.70	200.00	49521.55	1137.01	51146.69
99	4	99	371.41	312.52	200.00	49009.03	1508.42	51518.10
100	5	99	367.57	316.36	200.00	48492.67	1875.99	51885.67
101	6	99	363.70	320.23	200.00	47972.44	2239.69	52249.37
102	7	99	359.79	324.14	200.00	47448.30	2599.48	52609.16
103	8	99	355.86	328.07	200.00	46920.23	2955.34	52965.02
104	9	99	351.90	332.03	200.00	46388.20	3307.24	53316.92
105	10	99	347.91	336.02	200.00	45852.18	3655.15	53664.83
106	11	99	343.89	340.04	200.00	45312.14	3999.04	54008.72
107	12	99	339.84	344.09	200.00	44768.05	4338.88	54348.56
108	1	0	335.76	348.17	200.00	44219.88	335.76	54684.32
109	2	0	331.65	352.28	200.00	43667.60	667.41	55015.97
110	3	0	327.51	356.42	200.00	43111.18	994.92	55343.48
111	4	0	323.33	360.60	200.00	42550.58	1318.25	55666.81
112	5	0	319.13	364.80	200.00	41985.78	1637.38	55985.94
113	6	0	314.89	369.04	200.00	41416.74	1952.27	56300.83
114	7	0	310.63	373.30	200.00	40843.44	2262.90	56611.46
115	8	0	306.33	377.60	200.00	40265.84	2569.23	56917.79
116	9	0	301.99	381.94	200.00	39683.90	2871.22	57219.78
117	10	0	297.63	386.30	200.00	39097.60	3168.85	57517.41
118	11	0	293.23	390.70	200.00	38506.90	3462.08	57810.64
119	12	0	288.80	395.13	200.00	37911.77	3750.88	58099.44
120	1	1	284.34	399.59	200.00	37312.18	284.34	58383.78
121	2	1	279.84	404.09	200.00	36708.09	564.18	58663.62

Pmt No.	Payment Mo	Yr	Interest Portion	Principal Portion	Additional Principal	Remaining Loan Balance	Interest for Year	Cumulative Interest
122	3	1	275.31	408.62	200.00	36099.47	839.49	58938.93
123	4	1	270.75	413.18	200.00	35486.29	1110.24	59209.68
124	5	1	266.15	417.78	200.00	34868.51	1376.39	59475.83
125	6	1	261.51	422.42	200.00	34246.09	1637.90	59737.34
126	7	1	256.85	427.08	200.00	33619.01	1894.75	59994.19
127	8	1	252.14	431.79	200.00	32987.22	2146.89	60246.33
128	9	1	247.40	436.53	200.00	32350.69	2394.29	60493.73
129	10	1	242.63	441.30	200.00	31709.39	2636.92	60736.36
130	11	1	237.82	446.11	200.00	31063.28	2874.74	60974.18
131	12	1	232.97	450.96	200.00	30412.32	3107.71	61207.15
132	1	2	228.09	455.84	200.00	29756.48	228.09	61435.24
133	2	2	223.17	460.76	200.00	29095.72	451.26	61658.41
134	3	2	218.22	465.71	200.00	28430.01	669.48	61876.63
135	4	2	213.23	470.70	200.00	27759.31	882.71	62089.86
136	5	2	208.19	475.74	200.00	27083.57	1090.90	62298.05
137	6	2	203.13	480.80	200.00	26402.77	1294.03	62501.18
138	7	2	198.02	485.91	200.00	25716.86	1492.05	62699.20
139	8	2	192.88	491.05	200.00	25025.81	1684.93	62892.08
140	9	2	187.69	496.24	200.00	24329.57	1872.62	63079.77
141	10	2	182.47	501.46	200.00	23628.11	2055.09	63262.24
142	11	2	177.21	506.72	200.00	22921.39	2232.30	63439.45
143	12	2	171.91	512.02	200.00	22209.37	2404.21	63611.36
144	1	3	166.57	517.36	200.00	21492.01	166.57	63777.93
145	2	3	161.19	522.74	200.00	20769.27	327.76	63939.12
146	3	3	155.77	528.16	200.00	20041.11	483.53	64094.89
147	4	3	150.31	533.62	200.00	19307.49	633.84	64245.20
148	5	3	144.81	539.12	200.00	18568.37	778.65	64390.01
149	6	3	139.26	544.67	200.00	17823.70	917.91	64529.27
150	7	3	133.68	550.25	200.00	17073.45	1051.59	64662.95
151	8	3	128.05	555.88	200.00	16317.57	1179.64	64791.00
152	9	3	122.38	561.55	200.00	15556.02	1302.02	64913.38
153	10	3	116.67	567.26	200.00	14788.76	1418.69	65030.05
154	11	3	110.92	573.01	200.00	14015.75	1529.61	65140.97
155	12	3	105.12	578.81	200.00	13236.94	1634.73	65246.09
156	1	4	99.28	584.65	200.00	12452.29	99.28	65345.37
157	2	4	93.39	590.54	200.00	11661.75	192.67	65438.76
158	3	4	87.46	596.47	200.00	10865.28	280.13	65526.22
159	4	4	81.49	602.44	200.00	10062.84	361.62	65607.71
160	5	4	75.47	608.46	200.00	9254.38	437.09	65683.18
161	6	4	69.41	614.52	200.00	8439.86	506.50	65752.59
162	7	4	63.30	620.63	200.00	7619.23	569.80	65815.89
163	8	4	57.14	626.79	200.00	6792.44	626.94	65873.03
164	9	4	50.94	632.99	200.00	5959.45	677.88	65923.97
165	10	4	44.70	639.23	200.00	5120.22	722.58	65968.67
166	11	4	38.40	645.53	200.00	4274.69	760.98	66007.07
167	12	4	32.06	651.87	200.00	3422.82	793.04	66039.13

Pmt No.	Payment Mo	Yr	Interest Portion	Principal Portion	Additional Principal	Remaining Loan Balance	Interest for Year	Cumulative Interest
168	1	5	25.67	658.26	200.00	2564.56	25.67	66064.80
169	2	5	19.23	664.70	200.00	1699.86	44.90	66084.03
170	3	5	12.75	671.18	200.00	828.68	57.65	66096.78
171	4	5	6.22	677.71	150.97	0.00	63.87	66103.00

Amortization Schedule
Data Information Sheet
(This page may be photo copied)

Below is the information needed to prepare my loan payment schedule.

Original Loan Amount..............................$_____

Interest Rate..._____

Current Loan Balance............................$_____

Term (Number of Years).........................._____

Monthly Payment
(Deduct any insurance & taxes)................_____

Regular Monthly Pre-Payment.................._____

Name..

Address..

City, State, Zip..

Enclose your check for $12.00 and mail to:

> Back Home Industries
> P.O. Box 22495
> Milwaukie, OR 97222

Additional Resources from Back Home Industries
(This page may be photo copied)
Prices include shipping

_____ Copies of *A Banker's Confession* @ $11.95   _____

_____ One year subscription to our newsletter
The Home Instructor @ $10.00   _____

_____ *Advent Foretold* (Our December devotional)
@ $21.95   _____

_____ *God's Priceless Woman* (Wanda Sanseri's
Bible Study for women of all ages @ $21.95.
Group rates for 8 or more copies $16.00ea.)   _____

_____ *Teaching Reading at Home* (Supplement to
the Writing Road to Reading. Can be ordered
separately for $21.95 or used in conjunction
with Wanda's teacher training class.)   _____

_____ Free Catalog of all our materials

Send free information on our seminars:

_____ A Banker's Confession: Getting Out of Debt

_____ Money and Banking in the United States from a
Biblical perspective

_____ Teaching Reading at Home

_____ God's Priceless Woman

Send to: Back Home Industries
P.O. Box 22495; Milwaukie, OR 97222